Sister Suzie
Cinema

LEE BREUER

Sister Suzie Cinema

THE COLLECTED POEMS

AND PERFORMANCES

1976 - 1986

THEATRE COMMUNICATIONS GROUP

NEW YORK 1987

All inquiries regarding *Sister Suzie Cinema*, *The Warrior Ant*, and *Red Beads* should be addressed to Liza Lorwin, 360 West 22nd St., New York, NY 10011. All inquiries regarding *A Prelude to Death in Venice* and *Hajj* should be addressed to Mabou Mines, 150 First Ave., New York, NY 10009. *Hajj* appeared in earlier form in *Wordplays 3* published by PAJ Publications, New York, 1984. *Sister Suzie Cinema* first appeared in *Theater*, published by The Yale School of Drama.

Library of Congress Cataloging-in-Publication Data
Breuer, Lee.
Sister Suzie cinema

I. Title.
PS3552.R415S5   1987   811'.54   87-1955
ISBN 0-930452-60-7 (pbk.)

The photographs in this book are reproduced with the kind permission of the following: frontis, Ilaria Freecia; p. 54, Chris Ha; p. 68, Terry O'Reilly; p. 90, Chris Bennion; p. 104, Georgina Bedrosian and p. 126, Andrew Moor

Cover illustration by Michael Rocco Pinciotti.
Cover and book design by Joe Marc Freedman.

First Edition: January 1987

For Bill Spencer, 1927–1983.
Who brought music into my
Work twenty five years ago

So little can I accept
His death—I can't take his
Name out of my phone book.

Contents

THE POEMS

Sister Suzie

Cinema

Holy Saints Alive Sister Suzie
Are we ever moving pictures
Sister Suzie Cinema Holy Toledo
Are we ever a two shot, ever so
Close up through this night flight and
Ever after lap dissolve

Holy Casablanca Sister Suzie

Holy Moley Annette Funicello
Are we ever so eye contact
Holy Smoke there's lovey dovey
In your eye — and boogie woogie
In your other eye. (Can't see both
Your eyes together in this
Close Shot.) Pull Back Sister

Holy Cow Frances Farmer
Are we a sight for sore eyes

Haven't I seen you someplace before?
In a Process Shot through a snowy window
The Hybernska Ulice, March five, 1922
I, Czech and cautious, going by "K"
Remarking, (voice off-camera), "She needs
One room. Why did they build a city?"

Didn't the wind whip you for me
By appointment with Special Effects
Half past one at Highbridge, tail
Of your Sunday dress between your knees
For me, Danish and supercilious
By the name of Johannes (or some such)
On the third day of July (or thereabouts) 1834

Through this night flight
Here and there, now and then
Me here now and you there then
We, here and there, so mellow now
And then so drama—clouds that
Moon at the window over the wing
Like a rush of you. I'm numb with you.

Holy Love of God look at me
I'm transparent, full of waves
And fishes and breezes and birds—
Isn't this the height of it
Twenty-two thousand feet
And aren't you The End of it
You Non-Stop In-Flight First-Run
Feature with your earphones optional

O Stardust—do we ever come
By messenger dripping from the lab
Are we ever the rushes . . .

O Chickensoup, I'd recognize you anywhere
You headliner, sucker of my greaser cock under
An L.A. moonbeam called Chessman's Flashlight
Till you broke your glass jaw on my Brody Knob

O Veronica of the Lake
O Dolores of the Rios
O my Emerald Brody Knob

Sister Suzie try it again, you'll like it again
It's take sixteen, fifty-three, June, from the teaser

To surf you in the sunset, just to
Ride your tide—sweat, tears, blood
And vitamin E cream—back to the
Prime time star studded. Carry me
Back to the prime time star studded
You Natalie Wood you. Would you?

Sweet Love. All about that
How about that. O Holy Christ
Hollywood, I miss you when I
Close my eyes, when I blink
What can I do? I'm a love junkie
For you. Will I O.D. over St. Louis?

Jew Girl. Hey you. Arab Hair
You—Armenian Belly. Hey hey
Gypsy Warm Fingers asleep
On a pile of little brothers
Mother, my Mother. Grandmother
My Grandmother, each in their
Moment of their day. Russia, you
And Hungary your mouth. You,
French Eye—you are the loves
Of my lives (You Continentally
Acclaimed International Co-
Production Just Released). Let us
Do this thing—this heart fuck

I love you. I wed you. Change
The sheets to white and drink
White wine and come white come
Into the white night cup.

You are my hope, my trust, and my healing
Sister Suzie Cinema you are my last reel

I can't walk out on you
Honey, I'm glued to my seat
Have confidence. You're box office
You'll be alone no longer
I'll be there when the popcorn's gone

Lies!

I have
Nothing to
Hide: ninety
Nine, ninety
Eight

I'm depressed:
Cash request

I can take
Anything: three
Bills a week
Less the Social
Security
I'll pay you

Tomorrow: @
Five O nine

I'll pay you
The day after
Tomorrow: @
Six forty-two

I'll pay you half: @
A quarter (that's forty
By Friday. Then if I —
I know you *need it*
Would I try to rip you off —
Post date a check — *Hey*
It's in the mail — heads
Or tails

The day before yesterday
The truth put me to sleep
A hailstorm on my fingers
Did not wake me, nor a
Light shining in my eye
The prophet of loss sang too
Faintly. I heard not Scripture

Bad @ three eighty-nine: really
Bad @ five sixty-four
Beautiful @ four twelve: really
Beautiful @ all of the above followed
By zeros

The problem is cash
   That's a lie
The problem is cash flow
   That's a lie
The problem is flow
   Don't you know

I love you: @ peanuts
I now pronounce you
A pound of flesh
@ two nineteen a pound

Lies: a study in cost
Accounting. Lies:
All lies: all . . .

I have a spiritual life: package
Includes food, shelter,
Pediatrician, tuition,
Orthodontist, summer camp,
Loan, lawyer, bail, shrink,
Pension and ascension. Gravestone

Inscribed *Here Lies a Spiritual Life* @
One hundred and twenty-four
Thousand eight hundred forty twenty-two
(None of this is tax-deductible at present
But there's a bill pending) . . .

Lies: a history of
Expenditures. Lies
All lies: all . . .

Let's work together:
Over four thousand
In legal fees

I never felt
Like this before
I'll never feel
Like this again. Buy
One. Get the other
Free

I love you
Daddy: even; and
I love you Mommy:
Steven

Dear Jerri I want to write to you something about Perry
I don't know if I've ever met you I can't picture
Your face nor those of your children whose names Donna
Tells me are Brian David and Jill and so I really
Don't know who I'm speaking to only who I'm speaking of
Which is Perry when I knew him which was more than
Twenty years ago when he was a fraternity brother a
Double date partner boogie 'n' bongo co-wailer co-op
Cruiser and pure and simply a dear dear friend of mine
More than twenty years ago it's true and at the same time
It's incomprehensible lives change children are born

Careers are made unmade and made again people's
    addresses
Change their faces change even their heads change
The far out go straight and the straight get flaky
In one sense more than twenty years is like a lifetime
And in another it's an illusion nothing changes at all
I was in Bangkok and flew back via Hong Kong with a
Stopover in L.A. customs stuck a periscope up my ass
On an impulse I called Mervin Mandlebaum et voila
I'd picked up a thread I'd dropped twenty years before
Here was old Merv again pouring out his heart telling
Me how Donna had had a script optioned by Jay Jerome
Apparently it was already in development under Jay
There at U.A. they had an office in the Burbank Studios
With a stall shower I remember when she was Donna
Dienstag I remember how often she took a shower when
    she
Was working the point is not who his wife was fucking
    now
The point is Mervin opened up to me did this not presage
For Perry and I a refinding of each other too was it not
Foreordained written across every palm save that of fate
I was told the Perry became a brilliant periodontist
A wonderful provider and father even a coach of little
League ball of all this I can know no more than he of me
My life in New York on Avenue B and so the Perry that I
Speak of miss and mourn must be the Perry of that long
Ago he as essential to the re-creation of that glow that
Was my UCLA years as are they themselves essential to the
Fullness of my memory back there in Westwood West L.A.
A couple of valley boys wet behind the ears we pledged
Together a fraternity called Tau Delta Phi all this seems
Quaint now but then that was the fifties remember it
Was the rack and pinion of our lives Till Death Friends
Was the secret meaning of Tau Delta Phi we were
    whispered
This at our initiation and threatened with a fate worse
Than excommunication were we to tell well that old motto
Despite its naivete Greek letters that stand for English
Words has proved itself true not even true enough I feel
That I am Perry's friend and through him yours after
Death as well and so may I add my deepest condolences for
The passing of Perry Pearlputter to those of your other

Friends may my love borne on images of the past hold
Sway with you now.

> Donna your idea about
> Hitting Perry Pearlputter
> For that thousand dollars
> I owe you was a little late
> First of all it's not in
> The Valley it's on Yerba
> Buena in Bel Aire and second
> I got a prerecorded tape with
> The directions to his funeral
> I don't know what to tell
> You baby I was going to ask
> Him to go fifteen so we could
> Have some fun I wrote this to
> Jerri do you think it's the
> Right kind of thing if so
> Would you mail it to Jerri
> Pearlputter 24043 $1/2$ Yerba
> Buena Bel Aire put my return
> If not would you mind sending
> It to your agent I could work
> It into a treatment for Jay
> Jerri must be worth a mint
> I'd left my name on the answering
> Machine so I had to follow
> It up that's just common decency
> Do you like the writing I
> Stayed up all night and missed
> My unemployment appointment
> Now it's past noon and I've
> Got a hard on and I want to
> Fuck you @ twenty-seven forty-
> Five which is the New York State
> Department of Labor Unemployment
> Insurance Division Quarter Week
> Penalty.

You
Turn me on @
Two bits over
Drawn

I'm here to stay @
L Ten Eleven

I'm going @ seven
Forty-seven

I'm coming: pennies
From Heaven

This is
Embarrassing
Gratis

I'll get back
To you: time
And charges

And I quote, *"By the old-style calendar*
The new year will be welcomed in at midnight
An hour which is as memorable for me
As the time of my coming into the world

According to a custom established since childhood
I have always begun from that hour to conform
My life to a new program — which is:
> *Voluntarily to direct my manifestations*
> *In such a way as to attain the aims*
> *Chosen by me for the coming year*

This year I will set myself the task of concentrating
All the capacities present in my individuality
Toward being able to acquire by my own means
The sum of money needed for cleaning up all my debts

> *Then I shall begin to write*
> *But on the sole condition*
> *That henceforth I be relieved*
> *Of all concern about the material*
>   *conditions*
> *Necessary for my mode of life*
> *Already established on a certain scale*

> *But if for some reason or other I fail*
> *To accomplish the task I have set for myself*

Then I will be forced to recognize
The illusory nature of all ideas
As well as my own extravagant imagination

And true to my principles
Creep with my tail between my legs
(As Mullah Nassr Edin would say)
Into the deepest old galoshes
That have ever been worn on sweaty feet

I picture myself
Organizing a new 'Institute'
With many branches
But this time
Not for the harmonious
Development of man
But for instruction
In hitherto undiscovered
Means of self-satisfaction

A business like that
Would run as if
On greased wheels"

The Financial Question
G. I. Gurdjieff
@ $18.95 hardcover

My life
Sucks @ big
Bucks

There is a womb of air
   Between my feet and the floor
There is a womb of silence
   Between my voice and your ear
There is a womb of lies
   Between my mind and life

I'm a pea
In a shell game
Don't bet on me
Five'll get you three

Red Beads

I

THREE days before she was thirteen
The child came down to breakfast
Combed and clean, to find her father

Going upstairs with a copper tray.
On the tray was thin toast with the
Crust trimmed off, strawberry jam

And a bowl of milk. "Mother is pale"
Her father said. He knocked
On the bedroom door as soft as silk

Mother ate the strawberry jam
Right out of the spoon, and drank
The milk and left the toast

How pale she was with strawberry
Mouth and milk skin, pale as a ghost
Around her neck were red beads

"Keep your promise, Daddy dear.
When I'm thirteen the thirteen beads
Are mine to wear . . ."

   •   •   •

That night in her room she said
Her prayers by the light of a candle
Dipped in bay. Said her father as he

Tucked her in, "For what did you pray?"
"I prayed for my dog and my cat
And my bird. I prayed for my red beads

Ten plus three." "Did you pray for your
Soul!" "No, I forgot. Will you punish me?"
He kissed her hard and closed the door

And the wind came up out of the floor
The words of the wind in her Mother's
Voice came through the window into her ear

"Are you brave, child? Come outside. I have
Your birthday present here." She heard
Red beads falling, tinkling on the lawn

Her dog leapt through the window
Like an angel at a ghost. She
Heard him howl like the wind

Or was the wind like a howling dog?
"Daddy, save me, please," she cried
And pulled the covers over her head

And hid her face till the wind
Was mute and the beads were still
And her dog was dead . . .

II

TWO days before she was thirteen
The child came down to breakfast
Dressed in green, to find her father

Going upstairs with a silver tray.
On the tray were tiny cakes and
Cherry preserves and a pot of tea

"Mother is pale," her father said.
"But Father, you are paler . . ."
He put the tray down by the door

And took her hand and held it close
First to his heart, then to
His lips, then to his forehead

Birthdays, birthdays, flowers and weeds
Wind and lightning — thirteen beads
"Is that my mother singing, father

Back behind the door?" He hurried in
She ran away and hid all day
In the autumn field of harvest hay

•   •   •

She watched from the field and
She watched from the hill and she
Watched from the bank of the stream

All day long the house was still
Not a puff of smoke, not one
Leaf fell. And the sun went down

As if under a spell. And the beetles
Dreamed. "Daddy, come and find me —
I have your breakfast in a bowl

A fig, a pear, a lock of my hair
Tonight I'll pray to save my soul!
Daddy! Come and help me. Daddy!

Help me bury my dog." He came
At once with pick and spade. Suddenly
She was afraid. He spoke to her

"You take the tongue and I the tail
We'll throw her into the rocky shale and
Cover her with mud. And mark her grave

With a drop of blood. With a bead!"
All this my Daddy strangely said and
Quickly turned, "Now come to bed."

•   •   •

That night in her room she could not
Pray. She could not speak or
Even lay her head upon the pillow

It was wet with fever sweat
Can't sleep. Won't sleep. I'll
Bite my tongue. I'll pinch my feet.

Her cat jumped down with a tiny moan
Her bird rocked on its perch without
A sound. Then, like the shiver of an

Eyelash of a girl who starts to cry
Rain dropped out of a shivering sky
Her mother spoke again that night

"Come down to the basement, dear
I have a present for you here to
Celebrate your thirteenth year."

She heard a cry at the cellar
Door. And a sound like
Marbles over the floor. Like

Rats running up the wall. The
Child could not see at all.
Morning . . . . . . They found

In a cellar stall, her kitten
Curled into a ball. And small
Red marks where it was bitten

• • •

"Come to breakfast, father. Sleepy
Head! The sun is high. There's cream
In the pitcher and bread in the stove

And speckled egg pie and flowers
On the table set for two — just me and
You. Last night I had a fever."

"Daughter, Mother's so pale I dare not
Leave her. Bring plum jam on a golden
Tray and coffee, black, and stay away"

• • •

The child knocked at the bedroom door
"Mother and Father, it's a shame to treat
A daughter so who's not to blame

Who'll be thirteen on Hallowe'en. I am
A woman, Mother, just like you I want
My Daddy! I want my due — a house

Of joy and end to sorrow." Her mother
Said, "Not till tomorrow!" "Give me
My red beads, Mother!" "Not till

Tomorrow!" They lay there both so pale
So pale from tip of toe to top of head
"Father," she said. "My cat is dead!"

She buried her kitten in the ground
And ran so far she couldn't
Be found. Her father called all day

In the woods he'd call three times and
Stop to listen. Three times he'd call
And stop to sigh. Each time he called

She started to cry. "I'll never
Go back home," she thought. But deep
Inside her thinking was the deeper

Thing she sought. "I'll go back
One more time. At midnight
The red beads will be mine. . . ."

III

THE NIGHT before she was thirteen
No one came. She lay upon
Her back unkissed. How cold

Was her bed where once a dog
Had slept and where a cat had kept
A green-eyed vigil by her head

In the stillness of the night her
Father locks his bedroom door. She
Hears his footsteps to the bed

Make ripples on the floor. The
Night. A black pond. Each sound
Falls in like a stone. "He's afraid

To leave my mother. I'm afraid
To be alone." The sky outside her
Window. Was it blackest night?

Or brightest day? Or was it
Lightning without thunder? My God!
It's twelve! She had forgot to pray!

•   •   •

"Come to the attic, Daughter. It's the
Door at the top of the stairs. If you
Want the red beads that Mother wears!"

In the attic, in the shadow, in
The corner of her eye waited
Her mother, pale as morning clouds

Hair white as winter morning sky
"O daughter," said the mother
"Does it have to end this way?

Is passion's jewel for one to lose
And one to gain upon a given day?"
"O mother," said the daughter

"I did not make the rules
I made not women live for love
Nor made I men all fools"

Then she unclasped her mother's necklace
Never once did their eyes meet
And held it to her own white skin

Red beads like drops of blood
Upon a sheet. "Count them, daughter
Thirteen. Every bead is there!"

She wound them 'round the girlish
Throat and twisted! Whistling
Through the air the bird careened

From room to room to find the father
"Quick! Come quick! For it's your
Daughter's doom!" The mother gasped

"Here will begin my second life
I'll live again in you. Woman's
Born in blood. The child must

First go to her grave. You'll die
And I'll become the child again
While you become love's slave."

"Daddy! Save me!" cried the daughter
Necklace 'round her throat. But when
He came a pale young girl sat motionless

Remote. "Save me, Daddy. Save me"
How her voice had changed and how her
Eyes were burning and her heart deranged

Her father said, "You know the truth
The beads are yours. She was a witch
And I in thrall. Your mother's lost

We'll look for her. You know the truth
Once and for all. You and I dear
Daughter, we will hold each other

By the hand and vow a vow of fealty
To the rightful lady of the land." All
Hallow's Eve they search, the pair, the

Father dark, the daughter fair. "Mother
Is lost. Search low and high." But they
Never find her. The truth was a lie

Hajj

I

I sing of you, Alex, who I killed (of course I did)
And thank you, dear, for every fantasy I reaped
And curse you, cunt
        I owe you money

You've been dead for half my life. You are
My half life, love; you date my art
I see my art in the green glow of radium
Always less by half; I see this game
As cute as archaeology
        I'm gonna pay you

Baby, watch me dig you up
And stuff it up your sigmoid flexure
Watch me write this
        I sing of you

Once
Once a life wallpaper smokes
Yellow leaf clusters flare, fall, flake away
Under my bare, bathed footprints. Once
Once a life the clock, the demon reads aloud
The writing on the other wall
                    A call to pilgrimage

Ready or not, Alexis, here I come with cash
My check's no good, dead girl
I come to fuck you with a
                    Roll of Jacksons

Lo and behold we're on our way (follow the bouncing ball)
The sun looks like a melted Deutschmark; it acetylenes
The scenery — roads, rivers, rocks like crap on the
                    Ten below snow

I think of your ribs and your life in my mind
The sun goes out *ssst* like a match into a wave
We're on our way to Cheat's Bay *ssst* lights out
                    Let's drive in darkness

If I sell this Alexandra I will move your bones to Persia
Want to bet me, conqueress of Asia? Put your money
                    Where your mouth was

If only I can talk to you, Ali, lovingly

Here in the moon-blanched kitchen of my dreaming
Powder snow blowing in a genie gust

Or in the bathtub of my memory lit by nostalgia's candles
Shadows of cats on the shadowy walls chasing shadows of
                    Mice on the ceiling

If I can talk to you with a tongue fresh licked
By a tongue fresh licked I will be better
Every time a little better bled of pride
                    Alex . . .

You go dead on me. You are the one
I can't pay off; I can't put off your bill until

The day after tomorrow when I score
(I'll score for more the day I eulogize my owing)
Unhappily, you're through. There's just
no coming through for you (You done me
        See I ain't a good guy)

I can't suck my absolution from your collarbone
        And you can't cry

        Love is money Alex; money, love
        That's all ye need to know
        The terms . . .

        I owe you forty dollars
        Alexandra of the earth
        Now let's do business

I can't talk to you. I talk to money
Money knows me; we make deals
Throw me a line. I'll write it on you, Alex,
With my fingernail below your spine

        Once you die you live forever
        Once you've lived you're good as gone
        One's the billing, one's the fee
        Open your black box, baby
            Cash me in secrecy

II

How strange the night, Alexis, sleeping with you
In the Fourteenth Arrondissement, in the brass bed
(Fuck, the mummy bag on the echo stone in
Agamemnon's tomb—it was raining)
O non dimenticare, Alex. Sleeping with you
On the Via Fiorello under the Lambrettas
(Fuck, on the train to you, you beautiful Champagne,
Urbana). In the canyon (fuck, Coldwater Canyon)
In the hottub, under the water, in front of the fan
(Fuck, fire). On the roof (the floor) of west six seven
Push B three (fuck, east B at three push C on four)
        Behind a window on the snowy sky
        Into which so many blackbirds fly

I hear my music playing
I hear all my loves
They're singing, listen, Alex,
I hear what I'm saying, listen
All the prayer bells stopped
Ringing

Strange the night, Alexis, sleeping with you
(Fuck, you) on the set of Hotel Universe.
The keys to Hotel Universe are in my pocket
Under the mat (at the desk in an envelope)
By the flowerpot second from the left (fuck)
Right (fuck) left. The keys to Hotel Universe
On key rings with initials ABCDEFGHIJKLMNO . . .

I hear my music playing

On the keys to Hotel Universe. The key rings *1 2 3 -*
4 5 6 7   8 9 0 - 1 2 3 4 Hello, I hear you
You're the one that rings a little dead
The gray eye looking inward, blue eye
Darting from side to side. An ear *tick tick tick*
To the geiger counter of obsession, ear
To decay — the half life that fits the half life
Me half you

Your face appears in other faces
Eyes swim up in other eyes. Your touch
Touches me, it's other fingers. Your death dies
Tingaling in everything

Right here . . . I write. Here I come, back
In love with you again . . . again. Alexandra
Read my writing. Open your eyes Janus-headed
Ghost of girl called fear of life and fear
Of life to come

III

I love this room
I want to die in this room
And I would, had not I heard
This call to pilgrimage
This knot of God in my throat

Drop of God on my eyelash
This deep dreaming home
Where you're waiting
Floating . . .

Breathless body, face up, deep down, night lit
Pool, shadows of dancers passing purple.
Alex, you're chlorine blue. Blood
From your eyes — vines of rosebuds winding . . .
        The deep dream of murder. Alexandra . . .

Since you died I've loved a lot of hungry mice
My spring is bent from mouse decapitation
Tell me, why do mice all worship at the raw device?
What dim late shadow drowned your mousehole?
See it steal over your ears, and paint your tail
        With shadow hopes and shadow fears

Alex Lukin was nineteen the year she O.D.'d
In Mort Sahl's suite at the Embassy in Philadelphia
Last seen, changing her underwear (She had some
Expensive underwear in a cardboard box she kept
In my closet. She kept other things in other boxes
All over West L.A.) Six a.m. — she'd just popped in
        To change her underwear

White Olds, top down, parks, honks. Gardner McKay
Is sitting in it in his white pajamas.
A big white Samoyed is sitting in it too
All that white is sitting on red leatherette
Alex in hite underwear — they drive into the fog.
        Mort follows

        He didn't need her dying
        I'm the Dutchman
        Pandora. Die for me.

IV

Love is money, Alex
Money, love; and that's
Not all ye need to know
Ye need to know the
Flip-side of the coinage
Speculation . . .

That I find your grave by matchlight
In the winter. Fog lights on the river ice
I can't believe my eyes; the glow of amber
Glow of fire flowing underneath. Dear lady
O how deep we are

I want to kill and love
In the identical motion
In the identical word
In the identical devotion

I want not one impossible thing, but two
Out of not one impossible need, but two
Called not one impossible name, but two
I am not one impossible one, but two

Here in the dark box of my throat I bring you back to life
I rip you off

I penetrate you with my deadness so deep jointedly
That worms will see just how alive a corpse can be
Against my body, Alex, your charmed bones take on
A certain glow

You can't leave me; that plan has a flaw
We'll never sort each other's atoms out
We are under sentence of a Boyle's law
For hope's dispersal in chambers of doubt

The Warrior Ant

He can start anywhere,
   He can talk to the paper.
   He has reconnaissanced its corners

And licked its blue lines.
   The poison in the feast is
   subtler than tongue can tell.

How can he know this . . . ?
   Musics in the ear bewitch the word.
   How can he hear this . . . ?

The blind eye hole in the
   seeing eye ball burns right through
   the paper, sky, and cloud.

How can he say this . . . ?
  Let him write on this page
  with the sky blue rule

That burgundy's red rhyming,
  Let him write 'round the
  brown hole in black circles.

He can talk to you. O warrior ant!
  He can talk to the light
  through the ant hole in the paper night.

AN ANT CONCEIVED

I

Of you, O Warrior Ant, he sings:
  Father of Nations, Builder of Hills,
  Conqueror of Peanut Brittle,

Oracle of the moon-ribbed cricket's
  chirp, who, at the calling
  of a chemistry known as

Destiny's Marinade, waged
  ravenous and holy war ten years.
  Its names were Peppercorn of God!

And Lord of Millimeter!
  Hear of its birth, which
  was no less than miraculous!

(While being more than suspect)
  Hear of miracles and their conceptions!
  (suspicions and their perceptions)

In the conceit of the night
  of the nuptial flight of
  the virgin queens

II

On the noon of the night of the flight
  of the virgin queens begins the
  to and the fro of the branches.

This swishing and bending — now
  here is the story — receiving and
  sending, this thing of the calling —

Calling one to another:
  the callings by names and the
  callings of branches, to and fro

The *yes* and the *no,* that be nameless.
  O callings be nameless!
  O beautiful things!

III

O rain! O spontaneous sweet
  rising rain! O afternoon before
  the night the queens take flight!

The falling rain is as a curtain drawn
  across the rising rain, the rising rain
  is like a fountain in a cloud.

And like a juice upon the surfaces,
  a pool in the interstices —
  a juice, a pool, a fountain —

They appear so lovingly, the
  drops of the wetness are said to
  succor . . .

On the leaf and the fold does this
  wetness *succor;* on each pistil and
  petal — the drops of this wetness.

All parts of the earth smell of juices;
  each drinks down the other, when the
  drops of the wetness are said to *succor.*

IV

Here is the moment the light is divided
  I speak of the twilight, before flight
  and the thing of the choosing.

O terror! Terror of choosing the
  glow of the likeness, from the gleam
  from the darkness; the strands of sun

From strands of moonlight, streaming,
  called Light of Lights, and Lights
  of Seeming — the twi-lights, gleaming.

I speak of the combing out of light
  into its true colors; rains of light
  into the rains of water,

Mouth to mouth, like colored juices
  flowing. I speak of the wanting. I speak
  of love's haunting in this, the moment

Of the rain's-bow-ing. And the hearing
  of wings, virgins in flight
  singing at night. Virgin queens!

V

In the heart of the night of the
  flight of the virgin queens begins
  the beatings; the black beatings

With the colors of the auras ringed
  around. Begins the notes . . . Ah!
  The notations. And the poems! O poems . . .

Balm of angels and shit of flies.
  Oh balm . . . and ah shit!
  Begins Ohs! Begins Ahs! In the forms.

See the forms such as they are!
  See them performed! In so far
  as there are five — see five performances

Under the five roofs of heaven!
  In the heart of the forms such as
  they are: (they are the rubbings

And the scrapings and the claxings,
  they are the oowheegings and the
  tintinkings); such as they are

They are the percussions out of the
  center in concert through the realm.
  They are the languages the Gods speak.

They are the sweet nothings whispered by
  fluids in the ears of the airs.
  Or if you prefer — they are caressings

Of earths by the fingers of fires.
  Such as they are, they are God's
  body languages, called *the Wormings*

And Burnings and Floatings and Flyings
  on Earth and in Fire and Fluids and Air.
  I speak of holy languages as gifts

And my languages as payments, for toil
  in employ in translation of love.
  How they conspire. They conspire together

To bring forth the secrets. But in truth —
  The secrets are most perfectly spoken of
  as a speechlessness. Heard as silence.

O thou, silence — thou art love's
  roaring of mind. But thou, O black bleatings —
  Such as thou art, thou art love's heart.

VI

Now, it is common knowledge that the
  edge of night's surrounded by a wall
  of pain. But it is uncommon knowledge

That the wall is peach. Peach
  is the color of the blood of angels.
  And it is common knowledge

That love, that night, this discourse,
  with such a wall as I've described,
  acts like a prison. But it is

Uncommon knowledge that the prison's
  fleshy . . . peach and fleshy.
  There are white windows in these walls;

They are round and holy and they
  pour forth light, and at the center
  of each window is its dark gleam.

And it is not knowledge at all
  but an intuition, a secret, and a
  divining, that one can love

With such a power on this night
  that one can rise and
  hover high upon the wall,

That one can see right through
  a window in the wall of pain.
  One can see through it!

VII

Beloved! I speak not of walls
  but of faces like walls,
  high-boned peach fortresses.

(Peach is the color of the blood
  of angels.) A window in a wall of pain
  is an eye in the face of a beloved

And the gleam in the eye
  is the refraction of a flame
  of recognition in a heart below.

Around each dark gleam eyes pour forth
  a light beam. And as in no other
  beam of light, each wave and quanta

Goes not thither at all impossible speed
  but calls to the darkness, "O come hither,
  darkness, in your impossible need."

VIII

O shadow, O mother, O stronger
   than me, you are the soul's
   self-same dichotomy.

On the breast in a shadow of weakness
   lie; in a buckle of knees
   and a turning of ankles, fly.

Yea, though he walk, he falters.
   Yea, though he run, he falls back
   in the true arms of love.

O power, O lover, O deep
   mystery, you are desire's
   impossibility.

In the true arms, loved and lover
   wonder, "Who is holding you? Whose
   is the third arm under?"

Yea, though he walk, he falters.
   Yea, though he run, he falls back
   in the true arms of love.

IX

The night of flight of virgin queens
   is love in the eye of the beholder.
   And love in the eye of the beholder

Is death in the eye of the beheld.
   I speak for the drone, now,
   the beholder whose art is suicide.

How does it prepare its mind?
   It prepares its mind in the way of
   lightness; it thrusts from its mind

The weight of consequence. I speak
   for the drone, now, whose colors are
   cerise in blue: a life reflective

In a mode voluptuous, a childish life,
a life of art. I speak for the drone,
for the beholder whose art is suicide.

The materials of this art are not expensive,
the apprenticeship not long. Masters —
there have been but few.

And they, scattered and little known.
Charlatans, fakirs, mere craftsmen —
these have multiplied. Yet even so

The art of suicide has always ruled
the others. It rules over poetry. It
conquers music and vanquishes the dance.

It is said of this art — whose name
is *surrender*, that it is like
the cherry blossom over the blue wave;

So frail that it shivers even before
the storm, and seeks to fall
even before the elements dislodge it,

So as to give to the puff of wind
its fragrance, even as it gives
to the blue wave its flowery soul.

All that has been writ is writ
here of the beholder, a warrior
of the caste of drone,

An artist in its right,
a smaller life, when one considers
the multitude in the scheme.

X

But even as I speak for the ant
of its undoing. Conspiratorily, I
sing secretly of our renewing.

I sing of the moment of the love
of *it* that was *our* last beginning
for once-and-for-all time.

XI

"In the dead of night, in the secret
pocket of delight, I am borne
to be born. I am the permissions.

I am! In the laser of an eye. I am!
A white star seeding the black sky.
Remember the to and fro

Of the branches — sending and receiving?
Even then and there, secretly,
I sang of my conceiving."

XII

"Hooray! Here is a song
of celebration! 'It is coming!'
'A warrior is coming!'

All the angels cry, and all
flowers fly home to perfume the air.
'O welcome to me!'

And 'O welcome to me!' again!
I have begun us again in
a torrent and a blessedness"

XIII

On the night of the flight of
the virgin queens there was borne
to be born a warrior ant,

Perfect in the measure of its means.
Here follows its history:
Angels bore him to me, and now

Angels have borne him away. I was
his soldier, yes, that was me.
I was his spit, yes, and his polish.

I was his nib. And as his nib
  dipped in his spit and polish,
  I write you secrets of a language lost

And strategies for wars undreamed.
  May the light of the kingdoms —
  animal, vegetable, and mineral,

And Gods, yes, God's little light
  shine down to console me.
  He blew me away. Yes, he did.

AN ANT CONCLUDES

I

*"At the topmost reaches of
  the Sequoia tree, the world is
  profound beyond intelligence.*

*Here! O Ant, Here at this height!
  Here is the truth in the form
  of moisture! Here is a resound*

*Of thunder, and an enlightenment
  of rain, and here in each
  cloud is its proper cruelty.*

*In the blue light! In the blast
  of blue sky-lidded light, (which
  is inspiration), you will find*

*Your monastery hanging by a
  silken thread. Here, O Ant, life
  hangs by threads! Abide, O Ant,*

*And leave this world! Live out
  your life in this cocoon and here
  await the white moth of the moon."*

II

Abide it does and lives with Death
  in her pavilion in the sky until the
  time writ in the book for it to die.

III

And so a death moth becomes the
  ant's last lover. Death and the Warrior!
  Love is perfection, perfection of loves

Loved before; for of all the graces
  and delights of passions past,
  at core, what had not been

Death in them had been superfluous.
  In Death there was no competition,
  no contest for the goods of this world.

Death's needs were not in the
  realm of the goods. She hungered not
  for fame, fortune, or victory.

She was no searcher after self.
  How strange! She was the antithesis
  of all things ant-like. Yea —

As things create their opposites,
  the insect's death was born of the excess
  of life in it. As lover can discover

In itself, the self that is beloved,
  as one embracing arm can feel its strength
  according to the other's pressure —

So, to the ant, it was revealed
  that Warriors exist
  because Death loves them.

IV

The Warrior owes its very life
   to Death, who, despite herself,
   becomes dependent on the Warrior.

Such desperate attachments are a tragedy
   to see. Death lives in agony. She lies
   abed in her bathrobe all day long

Wiping tears and smoking cigarettes:
   smoking cigarettes and wiping tears and
   drinking water. A hundred times a day

She leaves him and a hundred times and one
   returns. How pitiful to see a moth
   addicted to the light; the light itself

Addicted to the darkness. And as each one
   struggles to become the other;
   once the other, back itself again —

So, this passion between moth and ant
   at times plumbs deep as an exchange
   of souls, each thrust upon the other

As a gift. At times it rests
   as shallow as an insect's grave where
   gift is only an exchange of roles.

V

For the ant, Death is a lease on life.
   Her demise restores him, her pain
   heals. *This love is sadistic!*

This love is not pure! Is it all
   a delusion? An ant can't be sure.
   What percentage of a falsehood

Is as good as true? What part of fact is
   just one's faith in it? The power of an
   ant's obsession rules summer's last days.

VI

The insect erects a tower of euphoria.
   (There is no upper limit to a
   tower of euphoria.) Life And Death,

Here, in the form of ant and moth,
   work against time. They will conceive
   new generations; they will mount

New campaigns, command new armies;
   (Not of ants alone! Of half the
   insect world! And of some vertebrates!)

The ant will heal its wounds. Miraculously,
   new antennae from its brow will sprout,
   and wings, again, will lift it high as aether.

VII

The cocoon becomes a shrine called
   The Pavilion on the Lake of Sky.
   Artists come and paint its holy history

On screens; these, in turn, in triptych,
   become ant ikons. *"Blessed are the Last Days
   of Summer in the Pavilion on the Lake of Sky."*

This is the title of the first screen.
   It shows Death, a late riser,
   basking in the sun as is her habitude;

On a green leaf, framed in the redwood
   branches, she drinks a delicious cup of coffee.
   After her coffee she opens her eyes.

(Eyes, like a filigree, cover her wings.)
   Death whispers, "Ant, I love you. Fly
   with me. Mine are wings of poetry."

VIII

On the horizon of the Lake of Sky
    there is a strip of silver. Turning in
    a circle, one can see it girds the world.

This is a bed of ice, and on it
    winter lies waiting. All summer's
    flowerings are held in this icy vase.

From her bed of ice, winter sends Death,
    her first snowflake. She alights like snow
    upon the living mouth and melts there.

This is the kiss of Death. But if, as now,
    it is too early for such kisses,
    Death melts in the sun with love.

IX

In the Pavilion on the Lake of Sky
    sunlight is rapt with itself.
    Golden clouds throw golden beams

Like golden fingers, down, to massage
    the earth right where it hurts. Such
    is the perfection that breezes hush,

And birds vanish, (sky brooks no
    movement), and violets beg shadows to
    hide them away. Summer suns and

Moons hang pendulous on cobweb strands;
    the strands creak with their tautness
    like overtuned instruments.

X

With love, it does not matter — day or
    night! Only flight matters. In these
    chosen hours, when, like orbed miracles,

Sun and moon shine together, ant and moth
   step out upon the meniscus curve
   of blue, depressing the sky's skin

Like bugs, the skin of water. They fly
   into the blooms of galaxies and suck the
   nectar therefrom. Yes, that is their food —

The firestorms, the drops that burn
   like comets on the tongue. Love of moth
   is love of ant's apotheosis.

Death is its darling; this Death is
   its own. Her wings, like two fellatio tongues,
   suck out its battlesongs and swallow.

Sweet soft core of inspiration! Now
   it knows! Death gets it off! Of course,
   the ant is mad (and a trifle sexist, too).

A Warrior, it confuses loving Death
   with conquering the thing.
   Yes, it confuses them . . .

XI

Of the curse called *Love of Death*
   so much has been written;
   and on the death of love, even more.

But what of the pain Death herself
   must feel for a living thing
   each time she takes one . . .

Each time she takes a life into
   her heart, the rush of blood
   and flood of mind destroy her.

Life tastes unnaturally sweet; Death's
   palate is accustomed to the tasteless.
   Each time she takes a life into

Her heart, her heart breaks over it.
   And broken-hearted she is brought, by stages,
   to unbearable loneliness and decline.

XI

The moth becomes a recluse.
  She falters and fades, languishing
  like a flower deprived of sun and water.

Only rarely does she speak,
  and then, with such a childlike and
  tremulous sound, the ant hears it

As the music of a harp of cobwebs
  dripped upon by dews. By day
  she cowers wide-eyed with confusion,

Her mind a litany of anguish
  and a sensibility deranged.
  "What should she wear?"

"How should she do her hair?"
  The ant is seized with dread;
  he cannot find her thread.

By night her eyes are wider still
  for as confusion starts to clear,
  the moth begins to suffocate with fear.

The pit is deep; its walls are slippery.
  She lives with terror in a trance.
  Her need for love is endless

(Fear burns love as a fiery fuel
  and the fires of the Death Moth
  are ever near extinguishing).

What could Death be afraid of?
  Alas, no thing can see with greater
  clarity than she, that love will lose . . .

XIII

Her wisdom comes upon her
  in an effect so curious; the
  moth dissolves in waves of light.

Death's dear face is insubstantial;
   her body waxes and wanes, it becomes
   translucent, and the ant sees through her.

The ant sees right through Death.
   So rare a sight is this, so few
   of all the living things have

Seen this that an insect sees.
   The ant can see the angel which
   an eye must look through Death to see.

It sees Death is of God's dominion,
   too, not an unholy thing;
   God's creature, too, is Death.

And the ant knows it shall die
   of pity. The story goes,
   "An Ant shall die of pity and love

For Her whom all the Saviors missed."
   O Compassionate Ant! How fitting!
   Death shall kill thee with her pain.

XIV

You are a child raised by women
   In your dreams, O child, like ant
   You live in a garden of beings

Like blooms and blooms like beings
   You give them names—Desire's Metamorphosis
   Sweet Bondage, Poisonheart

Infinitely small are you
   On flower petals, like the racked clouds
   You sprawl and sport yourself

Just like a dewdrop. Here,
   Oh Ant, the infinitesimal, like
   the weak, are earth's inheritors.

O subtle mind, thy name is Insect.
  In your dream you must be dreaming,
  Ant, even as you sleep you die

Mixed with water you'll be drunk
  as a tonic by the tree roots
  Subtleties revert to common cores.

Know that where love flowers so it withers
  Nature swears upon mortality and
  ants grow fickle in gardens of love

Know that inspiration is not in the bloom extravagant
  But in the flutter of the Death
  that rests on each one briefly.

A ghostly moth in passion's bloom carries
  Its soul up as the petals fall.
  Ant, it is at this same Death's door you knock

Gently, for it's late. The angel may be sleeping
  Howsoever much you long to spend the evil night
  You can't presume upon her ministry.

XV

There comes a night when even angels
  cannot sleep. They cry till all the
  clouds are burnt with falling stars.

(Falling stars are from the eyes
  of weeping angels. They are the
  grief of light drenching the sky pillow.)

On this night, Death, weeping, leaves
  the sleeping ant, and flies off like a ghost
  into the moon; to reappear with minions.

Clouds of moths as thick as snowflakes
  swirling out of the moon. O Ant!
  Winter's come! Snowflakes are falling.

By day they're black as ash. By night
  they're white, so you can see them
  in the sky without God's light.

XVI

O Warrior Ant! All wars are lost!
Your luck is gone and ghostly storms
are raging. While you're dreaming,

Death is falling. Who does she love?
Who is she kissing? Fool! You've
loved her so dearly you have won her.

Warrior Ant! Awake and flee!
What dreams do you dream! Dreamy
victories cannot your soul redeem.

XVII

The moth says to the ant,
    "I am the truth! And truth,
    I fear, you don't want to hear."

The ant says in its dream,
    "I do. Death Moth, I want you."
    And wedded to him by his words,

It's Death alights right on the leaf
    from which the tiny white cocoon
    hangs swaying. Inside, as in a holy cell,

The ant is sleeping. And the Gods
    in their Realms, and the beings on
    their planets ALL STOP EVERYTHING!

The wheel of Karma pauses till the truth
    be known. Can an ant attain enlightenment?
    Will the Warrior be the first among its kind?

No.

O Ant, you'll wake no longer to this world.
    May you awake upon the fingernail of the Almighty!
    May you carry your crumb of Heaven home.

XVIII

Death claims the Warrior Ant
    for he is now her own. Like two
    dreams dreaming of each other,

Ant flows into moth, moth into ant,
    across the line of void, until each
    annihilates the other with annihilating love.

The Death Moth and the Warrior Ant,
    like the touching of a plus and
    minus charge, vanish in mid-air.

And nature returns to herself,
    and in its own mysterious way,
    is tranquil. In the brittle bowl

That holds this summer's passions
    in a liquid form, a crack appears;
    The mold breaks. Summer of the Insects!

O you tiny drops of joys and
    even smaller sorrows — you leak away,
    leaving earth's autumn as a residue.

THE
PERFORMANCES

The Theatre and Its Trouble—An essay

I

1.   If a fact falls in the forest and you hear it not — is it a fact at all? Might it not have been your fancy? Theatre, *de facto*, did originate. I'm sure there was a time and a place. But I didn't have a ticket. And no one sent me the reviews. I'll content myself with truth according to the fanciful. Fancy, which is the soul of fact, makes fact ring true. And the truth is, theatre started with the wolves.

2.   Moon . . . mountain . . . snow blanket, snow pillow, snow sheet; the bed is coldly made, the table savagely laid, for a howling. Look! It is the moment of the turning around. *The turning around* was initiated in the theatre of the wolves.

3. Sing, O wolves, of wolfish mysteries. Why does one wolf turn around? Is one chosen? Does one sing better than the rest? Is one inspired by the wolf ghosts of wolf ancestors? Does one preach the wolfish word? We hear. We echo. We howl. We harmonize—we wolves.

4. Sing. Dance. Paint your faces. Don't ask an actor why. Ask a singing bird, a prancing peacock. Ask any fish who changes colors. Applaud the *mie* of Tomasaburo! Applaud the postures of lions.

5. Read your program. It is a genetic program.

6. Performance is the method of natural selection adopted by culture. Culture is society's DNA. Performance is fashion. Survival of the fashionable. That's what it's all about.

7. What is acting? Acting is the moment when, after *performance* turns around to the front, it turns back to the side.

8. And half facing you is half assing you. And that's the theatre and its trouble.

II

9. The girl I wanted was in pink pedal pushers and an aquamarine sweater and her name was Karen Bruce, and she was fourteen, and she was sitting on a metallic green, shaved, '49 Merc fender with my friend Larry Salk and she was having a Bob's Big Boy. And I—my head was down against the snakeskin steering-wheel cover—was watching her through my knitted dice. And a tear fell from my eye onto the sapphire shift knob; and I stuffed a french fry into my mouth and peeled out down the pavement like a fingernail on a blackboard. And when she heard my tires she knew it was my voice. And, naturally, time stopped and we fell in love forever.

10. What is this? Would it be naive, dangerously so, to suggest that this, in more scientific terms, in, say, field theory's terms, is a matrix of nostalgia experimentally verifiable by goosebumps from which, at any instant, a weak interaction called poetry could occur by the name of *Sister Suzie Cinema?* Yes, it would be dangerous. People have had their tongues, their cocks, their funding cut off for less.

11.   The danger—this being Theatre and Theatre spelling Trouble—is that poetry won't play.

12.   In order to better understand the problems of poetry in the theatre, take a little standard shift out onto the FDR and head uptown at about 4:45. When you pass under the Queensborough Bridge, shift into neutral and put your foot down on the accelerator hard. You glide to a halt. The motor whines. Feel the surge and the still-ness—pure poetry. Then a Cadillac rides up your bumper. The men in white coats come to take you away. The men in black leather jackets with badges reach right in your pocket. "Let me see your license!"

13.   What can you say. You can say, "Doctors! Officers! and Peers! I have no driver's license. I have a poetic license. Making poetry in the theatre is like learning to drive a standard shift. The key to not stalling is the foot on the clutch. The foot on the clutch down-shifts you from high-speed dramas with their actions, their characteri-zations, their suspense, their plot, their psychology—shifts you down through the gears of language—down, down, down to poetry. The motor goes faster and time goes slower and the power is greater and you use a hell of a lot more gas. And then you get to the poem itself. You get to that great gear of art called neutral, where the motor mind can rev to infinite tach, and the vehicle of time never moves at all. And then and there they book you. The charge is spiritual sodomy.

14.   The theatre and its trouble is that nobody wants to wait for poetry.

15.   No one minds waiting at the ballet or at the gallery. Tourists wait at scenic overlooks in the Smokies. But theatre has places to go and people to see and it cannot wait for poetry anymore than life can wait for dreaming. You have to trick it.

16.   I didn't tell you that back at Bob's Drive-In—all the way back in #9—the radio was on. Who was on the radio? Was it the Harptones? Was it the Moonglows? Was it the Platters? Fourteen Karat Soul, who sings *Sister Suzie Cinema*, is heir to them all.

17.   Music makes theatre wait for poetry. Sister Suzie's *food of love* was soul food. R and B was love to me. Doo-Wop was the *top down and the radio on* of this poor sucker's lyric muse. For this poor sucker, *In the Still of the Night* will always be where it's really at.

A 1982 performance of *Sister Suzie Cinema* at Riverside Studios, London featuring Fourteen Karat Soul, from left to right: Reginald "Briz" Brisbon, Russell Fox II, Glenny T., Bryan "Le Mont" Simpson and David S. Thurmond.

Sister Suzie

Cinema

Sister Suzie Cinema, *a project of Mabou Mines, premiered in June 1980 at the New York Shakespeare Festival's Public Theater. Lee Breuer's poem was set to music by Bob Telson. It featured Fourteen Karat Soul, which was composed at that time of Glenny T., tenor; Russell Fox II, baritone; David S. Thurmond, countertenor; Bobby S. Wilson, tenor; and Reginald "Briz" Brisbon, bass. Ben Halley, Jr. was the Phantom of Doo-Wop. Sets were by L.B. Dallas and lighting by Julie Archer. Sister Suzie was produced by Liza Lorwin on tour in Europe and the U.S.*

In 1986, Sister Suzie was produced by KCET-TV in Minneapolis for the PBS series Alive from Off Center. *It was directed by John Sanborn.*

The stage is a "Pantages" of passion, a "Bijou" of dreams and a "Roxy" of romance. Saturday night finds the BROTHERS *(Fourteen Karat Soul) sitting in the back row of the late show. The movie begins. They are silhouetted in the projector light. They're eating popcorn.*

Setting the scene for us is the PHANTOM OF DOO-WOP, *resplendent in white tie, cape and tails. Sitting in his private red plush box at the edge of the stage, he adds just that measure of highbrow elegance we need for a night at the Doo-Wop Opera.*

The PHANTOM OF DOO-WOP
telis us:

On a Saturday night
In the June moonlight
An a capella Doo-Wop Group
From Guadeloupe
New Jersey
Is into seeing something
Groovy . . .
In the manner of
A movie . . .

The BROTHERS **sing the
"Suzie Vamp" and over it
we hear the "Bass Rap"**

It came together
Me and my movie
How could I falter
With you as my lead?

I went to a late show
And sat in the back row
And played with my yo-yo
And let my heart bleed

The BROTHERS **sing "Sister
Suzie Cinema"**

Sister Suzie
Sister Suzie Cinema
You're my movie
Movie star

You're my star bright
You're the first star I see tonight
How I wonder
Who you are

Sister Suzie
Sister Suzie Cinema
Cut my heart out
Silver knife

Holy holy
Holy holy moley girl
Set my soul free
Save my life

**The lead changes from
baritone to tenor**

You're my first run feature, baby
You come after Mickey Mouse
You're love's sweet teacher, baby
You sell out my house

I'll watch you forever, honey
I'll sit here all through the night
Just to play that scene with you again
The one in the moonlight

And back to baritone

Sister Suzie . . .
Wish I may and wish I might
Have the wish I wish
Tonight

**The "Suzie Vamp" again,
and over it a "Pledge My
Heart Rap"**

Holy Saints Alive Sister Suzie
Are we ever moving pictures
Sister Suzie Cinema Holy Toledo
Are we ever a two shot, ever so
Close up through this night flight and
Ever after lap dissolve

Holy Casablanca Sister Suzie

Holy Moley Annette Funicello
Are we ever so eye contact
Holy Smoke there's lovey dovey
In your eye — and boogie woogie
In your other eye. (Can't see both
Your eyes together in this Close Shot.)

Holy Cow Frances Farmer
Are we a sight for sore eyes

And then another "Bass Rap"

Hey hey French eye. Hey you
Arab hair. Mexico your mouth
Hey hey Gypsy warm fingers
You are the loves of my lives
(You continentally acclaimed
International co-production just
Released)

Here the BROTHERS leap-frog over the orchestra seats to the front row

Let us do this thing . . .

The baritone lead gets down on his knees

Sister Suzie
Sister Suzie Cinema
You're my first reel
My last chance

Can you hear me
Suzie can you hear my plea
Be my fantasy
My romance

The PHANTOM, in his role as the Clifton Fadiman of Doo-Wop, rises in his box and asks:

Who do you want
On a Saturday night
Who do you Doo-Wop
In projector light

If you want to know
The answer, Bro . . .

Come to the back row
At the late, late show

The BROTHERS "come on"
with the "feature"

Haven't I seen you
Someplace before
With John Barrymore
1922

Didn't we kiss
On a rocket ship
On some interstellar trip
With R2D2

They rap and clap

I'd recognize you
Anywhere, you
Headliner, you
Bright shiner, you
Bobby sox, you
Vernal equinox, you
Kahlua on the rocks, you
Twentieth-century fox

Sister Suzie, try it
Again, you'll like it
Again. It's Take
Sixteen, fifty-three,
June, from the Teaser

The BROTHERS sing "Prime
Time." The row of seats
they're sitting on rises right
up into the air — imagination
has "taken wing"

Carry me back
To the prime time
Star studded
You Natalie Wood, you
Would you

The row of seats is balanced
on a silver 727 airplane
wing. It rises over the
orchestra seats, jet engine
radiating laser beams,
spewing vapor trails of dry
ice across the night-blue
clouds projected in the sky

Carry me back
To the prime time
Star studded
You Natalie Wood, you
Would you

To surf you
In the sunset
Just to ride
Your tide
Sweat, tears, blood
And vitamin E cream
Back to the
Prime time

The BROTHERS take off! Wing strobes flash red and blue. The seats collapse right into the wing, becoming ailerons

Carry me back
To the prime time
Star studded
You Natalie Wood, you
Would you

To park you
In the moonlight
To cool you
By the pool
To pass your ass
On the Pasadena freeway
On your way
To school

Microphones sprout and footlights gleam along the wing. The BROTHERS are transformed! Off come the street clothes. Underneath are white silk jumpsuits, silver bomber jackets, sky-blue scarves, rose leather shoes

Carry me back
To the prime time
Star studded
You Natalie Wood, you
Would you

The PHANTOM OF DOO-WOP says:

Fasten your seat belts!
Put out that fag!
Stick your face in the oxygen and
Take a drag!

Suzie makes these guys so high
She's like an in-flight movie in the sky
Now, Fourteen Karat's hearts will sing
While Fourteen Karat's Souls take wing.

He breaks out a score and a baton and goes to work

The BROTHERS sing "Night Flight"

Through this
Night flight
Be my
Bright light

Through this
Night flight
Hold my
Hand tight

The wing rises up into the
flies, and having "attained
the heights," it banks

Through this
Night flight
Here and there

Through this
Night flight
Now and then

Through this
Night flight
Through the air

Through this
Night flight
Right to the end

Below, dry ice clouds
envelop the PHANTOM OF
DOO-WOP up to his waist.
Losing the score which he
has been following, he dives
into the cloud to find it and
disappears

Look at me
I'm numb with you
I miss you when I
Close my eyes

     This is the
Height of it
Ten thousand feet
How my mind
Flies . . .

Hollywood
Love so good
You make me
High

Then reappears like a
porpoise out of a sea-cloud
as he retrieves the lost pages

Feels so good
My oh my . . .

Through this
Night flight
Be my
Bright light

**Galaxies spin and comets
flash on a projected
firmament. Tiny rainbow-
gelled pin-spots play over
the singers in a syncopated
twinkle**

Through this
Night flight
Hold my
Hand tight

On this
Jet stream
Where my
Soul dreams
All the
World seems
To be
Moon beams

Through this
Night flight

**The silver wing banks at
forty-five degrees. The
"moon glows." The
BROTHERS sing the riff and
ride it out**

Sweet love
What about that
How about that!

**The bass man goes down on
the wing and hangs over
into the stratosphere. On
the "Wing of Love" space is
a wet dream**

Through this night flight
Here and there, now and then
Me here now and you there then
We, here and there, so mellow now
And then so drama — clouds that
Moon at the window over the wing
Like a rush of you. I'm numb with you.

**The BROTHERS fly under the
constellation "Sister Suzie."
This is the "Bass Rap"**

Holy Love of God look at me
I'm transparent, full of waves
And fishes and breezes and birds —
Isn't this the height of it

Twenty-two thousand feet
And aren't you The End of it
You Non-Stop In-Flight First-Run
Feature with your earphones optional

O Stardust — do we ever come
By messenger dripping from the lab
Are we ever the rushes . . .

And the riff swells up and out

Sweet love . . .

Time stops; music stops. Comets freeze in their tracks. One face looks longingly; one voice whispers the "Zap Rap"

O Veronica of the Lake
O Dolores of the Rios
O Sister Suzie . . .

You girl. Arab hair
You — Armenian belly
Hey hey Gypsy warm fingers . . .

You are my hope, my trust, and my healing
Sister Suzie Cinema you are my last reel

I can't walk out on you
Honey. I'm glued to my seat
Have confidence. You're box office
I'll be there when the popcorn's gone

And with an a capella arpeggio everything starts up again — that is, everything comes down again. The BROTHERS sing "I'll Be There when the Popcorn's Gone"

You are my hope
My trust
And my healing
Sister Suzie
Cinema

The wing levels and begins its descent, landing, strobes flashing, a London blitz of searchlights — pink, green, yellow, violet, blue

You are my last reel
I can't walk out on you
Honey I'm glued to my seat
Have confidence
You're box office baby

There's someone to save you
'Cause I'll be there
When the popcorn's gone

Everybody has his popcorn back. They pelt the audience with popcorn balls. A choreography of "half court" moves – the back pass and the sky hook and the 'ol one-handed push

Sing it to me
Sandra Dee
Once more with feeling.
I'm the pretender
I surrender every night.

You are my last reel
I can't walk out on you
Honey I'm glued to my seat
Have confidence
You're box office baby
There's someone to save you
'Cause I'll be there
When the popcorn's gone

O Sister Suzie
Look at me again
Don't you walk into that sunset
Don't you let my movie end

The lights are low
And I'm feeling oh so high
I will never, never
Never, never say
Bye-aye! Bye-aye!

You are my hope
My trust
And my healing
Sister Suzie
Cinema

You are my last reel
I can't walk out on you
Honey
I'm glued to my seat
Have confidence
You're box office baby

There's someone to save you
'Cause I'll be there
When the popcorn's gone

Back in his box, the
PHANTOM OF DOO-WOP **stands**
up and jives with the
BROTHERS. **Call and response**
pattern

Yeah Yeah

Because I'll be there
When the popcorn's gone

With all manner of campy
ad-libs

Don't believe that one. I know him!

Baby, I'll be there
When the popcorn's gone

They'll be gone. And the popcorn will be gone.
And you'll be miserable. Miserable!

Rubato and ornamental

No no I'll be there —
When the popcorn's —
Gone —

The PHANTOM OF DOO-WOP
takes out his handkerchief
and cries:

I believe you. I believe you.

The BROTHERS **sing a reprise**
of the "Sister Suzie Vamp"
and over it the bass man
raps:

It came together
Me and my movie
We opened up uptown
On Fifth Avenue

We played it light
As a feather
Then we played heavy
In leather

Then we came
Together
And my movie
Came true

END

III

18. Poetics is the foreplay of science.

19. *Ham's Law* or the *First Law of Thespodynamics* states that in the case of the one or several facing another one or several, the *fewer* are the *more meaningful* than the *greater* in inverse proportion to the square of the difference between the two. Implied in the equation is a reduction of the ratio to a point where *one* faces *everyone else* and is, by inverse implication, *the greatest*. In the language of Thespodynamics, the greaters are known as the *hearers* and the lessers as the *sayers* – and the process as *hearsaying* – except in the case of a reduction to one – in which case the lesser is known as *the ham*.

*Saying and *hearing* is the pretty pass that *calling* and *responding* have been brought to. See VI, 44-63.

**When unions are involved *hearsaying* is known as *gainsaying*.

20. There follows from this a second law known as *The Gross. The Gross*, and its corollary *The Net*, concern the interaction of forces between hearing and saying when they are reduced to *The Numbers. The Net* is a mystical number known as *Life Itself*.

21. There are weak forces and strong forces and gravities and electromagnetics – between hearing and saying, all that shit is involved – all those "matters" and "anti-matters" at the heart of the real showbiz. The force of the saying both attracts and repels all who hear it. And the act of the hearing itself can repel and attract what is said. And in this interaction known as suspense, a holding pattern can be found that determines all the shapes and the configurations of the theatre we know. This is the law of *Size of House*.

22. The name of the first force is the *killer* force, as in *Kill 'em dead, man;* the name of the second force is the *lover* force, and this force cries *bravo* and weeps. The killer and the lover forces are volatile. Alone they burn. Mixed they explode. And that ain't hay. That's Hegel.

23. Brecht! Marx! Science! Ha! The theatre and its trouble is its misappropriated dialectics. We are a study in dialectical dematerialism.

24.   Theatre is a special case of *performance* concerned with demonstration in pro-file. (See #8; characters are behaviorist profiles and they know it. Try and look one in the eye.) It demonstrates the world according to illusion against a scrim of the world according to the void. Through this scrim dialectical light plays.

25.   From the moment I first saw and fell in love with the Bunraku in Paris I thought that it, not Noh, was the true poem of the stage. For psychology was automatically perceived formally, the literal was automatically abstract. The more prosaic the idea the more poetic it became. To see a Bunraku puppet dance was, frankly, nothing much. But to see one take a piss was an epiphany.

26.   In Bunraku, traditionally, the master puppeteer is not hooded. Through its pain, ecstasy, through anger, grief, the puppet is manipulated with apparent impassivity, belied only by the master's eyes. Like the car on the FDR, the wheels never turn but a great hand moves it along above the flow of traffic. In *A Prelude to Death in Venice,* Bill Raymond manipulates a puppet of himself named John. It looks exactly like he's driving. But all is still.

27.   The manifestation of the illusion of life in something demonstrably dead is an existential sermon. All the lesser dialectics, the little Brechtian distancings, they are the openers for the real rock and roll—they are the Monkees for the Stones.

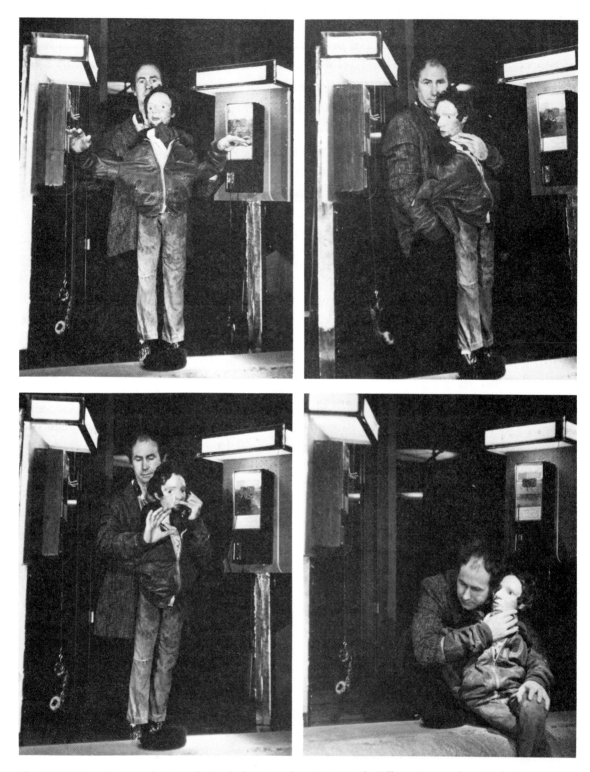

The 1979 Mabou Mines production of *A Prelude to Death in Venice* with William Raymond and "John" the puppet.

A Prelude to Death in Venice

A Prelude to Death in Venice *was produced by Mabou Mines and premiered at the New York Shakespeare Festival in May of 1980. It featured Bill Raymond, with Greg Mehrten as the Voice. The puppet, John, was by Linda Hartinian, the set by Alison Yerxa and L.B. Dallas, and the lights by Julie Archer. The music was composed by Bob Telson. Dyin' to Be Dancin' reached number six on the disco charts.* Prelude *was first published in* New Plays USA 1 *(TCG, 1982).*

On the street at night, JOHN GREED, *a puppet manipulated by* BILL, *stands at two touchtone* PAY PHONES *designated* I *and* II. *In front of them, a curb.* JOHN *wears a leather bomber jacket, levis and a blue knit watch-cap.* BILL's *voice is* JOHN's *voice as well as his own.* BILL *is dressed in a similar though not identical way.*

BILL, *as the puppet* JOHN, *dials* PHONE I.

JOHN (*On* PHONE I): "Johns Anonymous." Well, look in the commercial listings . . . Manhattan . . . thank you. (*Hangs up and dials again. It rings*) Hello, this is John . . . Hang on a sec . . . (JOHN *dials* PHONE II, *then continues on* PHONE I) Hi . . . Oh pretty good. Yeah . . . I got the card about the meeting, but I was overloaded at the time. Yeah, work . . . hang on a sec . . .

JOHN (*On* PHONE II): Hi. Oh. I didn't know it was that late. No, I don't have a watch. I have an electric alarm clock. Well, I was just out on the street and I thought I'd drop over. I woke up your kittens?

JOHN (*On* PHONE I): I can't do it!

JOHN (*On* PHONE II): Hang on a sec . . .

JOHN (*On* PHONE I): Hi. Sorry. I can't do it. No. I read that book. Right . . . the J.A. manual. That's a lucid book. You know what I'm saying? That's a work book. Right. It's about work — you know what I'm saying, "No!" Right. I'm saying, "No!" You know what I'm saying? My thing is not about work; my thing is about a vacation. In my life, at a critical juncture, I vowed not to work another day in my life. No. That's not the point. The point is, "I *can* work, but, I can only work when it's a vacation from a vacation." You know what I'm saying? I'm saying, "I can't do it!" It just ain't tourism. Hang on a sec . . .

JOHN (*On* PHONE II): Hi. Sorry. When did you have kittens? You didn't have kittens the last time I saw you. No, you were unattached. No, that's not the point. The point is, "You had kittens and you never called me." (*Hangs up*)

JOHN (*Turns to* BILL): You got a dime? (JOHN *reaches into* BILL's *pocket and finds a dime*) Thanks, man . . .

JOHN *dials* PHONE II *and speaks on* PHONE I *while* II *is ringing.*

JOHN (*On* PHONE I): Hi. Sorry. What do you mean, "I'm in bad shape"? I've been working out. What? "Work in"? You don't know what you're asking.

Simultaneously the answering machine begins on PHONE II.

JOHN (*On* PHONE I, *continued*): You know what I'm saying?

PHONE II (*Answering machine*): Hi! I'm not at home right now, but, if you'll just leave a message when you hear the beep of the tape, I'll get back to you just as soon as I can. Thank you. (*Beep*)

JOHN (*On* PHONE I): Hang on a sec . . .

JOHN (*On* PHONE II): Hi. This is John. If you play your tape when you get home, why don't you come over? You could just hop in a cab and . . .

PHONE I (*A recorded operator*): This is the operator. Your time is up. Please deposit another five cents or your call will be automatically disconnected. Thank you.

Recording repeats while simultaneously JOHN *speaks on* PHONE I.

JOHN (*On* PHONE I): What? I'm on the street!

JOHN (*On* PHONE II): Hang on a sec . . .

JOHN (*On* PHONE I, *over recording*): You'll call me. (*The phone booth light blinks off*) I don't know the number. Hang on a sec . . .

JOHN (*To* BILL): You got the number?

JOHN (*On* PHONE I, *over operator recording*): I can't read the number!

JOHN (*To* BILL): You got a light?

BILL *hits the* PHONE. *The light blinks on.* PHONE I *clicks dead. Then dial tone.*

JOHN (*On* PHONE II): Sorry. Now remember, the buzzer doesn't work, so I'll put a key in a luminous sock. When you . . .

Dial tone.

JOHN (*To* BILL): You got a dime? (*Takes dime*) You got another dime? (*Takes another dime*) Thanks, man. Thanks, man. (HE *inserts dimes in* PHONES I *and* II *and dials them simultaneously*)

JOHN (*On* PHONE I): Hi. Sorry. I'm having a seizure.

PHONE II (*Answering machine*): Hi. I'm not at home right now, but, if you'll just leave a message when you hear the beep of the tape, I'll get back to you just as soon as I can. Thank you. (*Beep*)

JOHN (*On* PHONE I, *continuing over tape on* PHONE II): A seizure, that's all. You don't understand — I live on the edge. You're coming for me? Right. I should stay glued to the corner. I don't recall the name of the corner.

JOHN (*To* BILL): Do you recall the name of this corner?

JOHN (*On* PHONE I): Hang on a sec . . .

JOHN (*On* PHONE II): I neglected to mention . . . uh . . . Why don't you bring a bottle of V.O.? Or a bottle of J.D.? Or a bottle of V.S.O.P.? A couple of steaks, some Idaho potatoes, iceberg lettuce, and polyunsaturated vegetable oil. I've got the vinegar. (*Hangs up*)

JOHN (*On* PHONE I): Hi. Sorry. I can't recall the name of the corner. I'll hang on.

JOHN (*To* BILL): You got a dime?

JOHN (*On* PHONE I): You know something — "Once I was a nothing." Isn't that something?

JOHN (*To* BILL): Thanks, man.

JOHN (*On* PHONE I): No, I don't recall the details. My life had escaped my notice, so to speak. I was such a nothing I was in a state of illumination. I knew the *trip*. I knew the *bit*. I knew the *man*. I even knew the *number*.

PHONE II *rings.* JOHN *answers.*

JOHN (*On* PHONE II): Hi. How'd you know my number? I'm an unlisted number. I don't even know my number. (*Hangs up* PHONE II. *Dials* PHONE II)

JOHN (*On* PHONE I): Now what I'm saying is, "Put yourself in my position. If you knew what I knew — wouldn't you know you needed a vacation?"

PHONE II (*Answering machine*): Hi. I'm not at home right now . . .

PHONE I (*Operator*): This is the operator . . .

PHONE II (*Machine*): . . . but, if you'll just leave a message when you hear the beep of the tape . . .

PHONE I (*Operator*): I have an urgent call waiting . . .

PHONE II (*Machine*): . . . I'll get back to you just as soon as I can . . .

PHONE I (*Operator*): Go ahead please . . .

PHONE II (*Machine*): Thank you. (*Beep*)

JOHN (*On* PHONE I): Get you a mango? Did you finish the sour cabbage? Good. Good. Just checking.

Tape on PHONE II *beeps again.*

JOHN (*On* PHONE I, *continued*): Hang on a sec . . .

JOHN (*On* PHONE II): Would you mind bringing a plunger — the john is backing up. I wouldn't ask you, but since you're taking a cab . . . you know what I'm saying . . . (*Hangs up*)

JOHN (*On* PHONE I): Where would I get a mango? The fruit market on the corner. What corner? My corner! (*Looks around*) Yes, as a matter of fact there is a small fruit market on my corner.

JOHN (*To* BILL): Got a dime?

JOHN (*On* PHONE I): That's not the point. The point is my aforementioned point . . .

JOHN (*To* BILL): Thanks, man.

JOHN (*On* PHONE I): . . . How'd you know my corner? I don't even know my corner. No. Well, it's late. Yeah. Work. Yeah. You could take a cab? Why take a cab? You live upstairs. Oh . . . you find it stimulating. (HE *dials* PHONE II *while talking*) You go uptown, and come back down the East River Drive. I never knew that. I don't want a club steak. I know you know how to fix the toilet. I'm saying, "*No!*" You know what I'm saying?

JOHN (*On* PHONE II): Hi. Sorry. We got cut off.

JOHN (*On* PHONE I): No, I'm not cut off. I'm the one that's connected. You're the one that's cut off.

JOHN (*On* PHONE II): No, you're not cut off.

JOHN (*On* PHONE I): I can hear it in your voice — you're ironical.

JOHN (*On* PHONE II): As I was saying, "Wouldn't you know you needed a vacation?" No, I'm not ironical. What I'm saying is, "*A trip!*" You know what I'm saying?

JOHN (*On* PHONE I): I love you too. Yes I do. Don't tell me, "No I don't!" Yes I do! Yes, I do have a heart on. Mother, don't be insecure. Mother, I don't want you taking a cab with a head of lettuce and a bottle of V.O. at this time of night. People will talk. That's not the point. The point is, I've been a closet mother fucker for years and I'm not about to come out now. Why? Because I'm innately conservative.

JOHN (*On* PHONE II): "A trip!" That's what I'm saying. "All work and no play makes John a dull Dick," so to speak. Am I getting over your head? Good. Good. Just checking. Hang on a sec . . .

JOHN (*On* PHONE I): Hi. Mummy . . . I'm terribly sorry. I can't be too careful. I've applied for a TWA Getaway Card. I'm sorry. Don't tell me, "I'm not sorry." I'm sorry!

JOHN (*On* PHONE II): Hang on a sec . . . sorry . . .

JOHN (*On* PHONE I): I said, "Don't tell me I'm not sorry." I'M SORRY!

Holding a receiver in each hand, JOHN *hangs up* PHONE II *by mistake.*

JOHN (*To* PHONE II): Sorry.
JOHN (*To* BILL): I really am sorry.

PHONE II *rings.* JOHN *answers.*

JOHN (*On* PHONE II): Wrong number!
PHONE II (*Mercury Message Answering Service*): Sorry.

JOHN *hangs up* PHONE II. PHONE II *rings.* JOHN *answers.*

PHONE II (*Mercury Message*): John, this is your number.
JOHN (*To* BILL): Is this my number?
BILL (*To* JOHN): Just do your number.
PHONE II (*Mercury Message*): John, your Dad called. Have you got a pencil?
JOHN (*On* PHONE II): Hang on a sec . . .
JOHN (*To* BILL): You got a pencil? (JOHN *takes a pencil from* BILL's *ear*) Thanks, man.
JOHN (*On* PHONE II): O.K. Shoot!

PHONE II *receiver shoots* JOHN *in the head.*

BILL (*Over "dead"* JOHN): Alas, Poor john . . . (*To audience*) Sorry. Hang on a sec . . .
BILL (*On* PHONE II): Pop, don't shoot the talent. It's very expensive to repair. I'm speaking frankly; you do — and we sue.
BILL (*To audience*): Sorry. Hang on a sec . . .

BILL *reanimates* JOHN *and resets receivers of* PHONES I *and* II. *Both* PHONES *ring simultaneously.*

JOHN(*Answering* PHONE I): Hi. I hung you up? Sorry. I was on the other phone. Oh, just shooting the shit.

PHONE II *continues to ring.*

JOHN (*On* PHONE I, *continued*): It was my service — Mercury Message Service. They're very good; they successfully transmit the flavor of the communication. Mummy, Dad's mad. Mummy, every chance he gets he wants to shoot me. He wants to shoot in Greece. Oh, you know, I'm supposed to kill my mother and marry my father. I don't want to shoot in Greece. I want to shoot in Venice. Hang on a sec . . . (JOHN *answers* PHONE II)

PHONE II (*Mercury Message*): John, Tom called.

JOHN (*On* PHONE II): Did he leave a number?

PHONE II (*Mercury Message*): Eighteen seventy-five to nineteen fifty-five.

JOHN (*On* PHONE II): Any message?

PHONE II (*Mercury Message*): Got a pencil?

JOHN (*To* BILL): You got a pencil? (JOHN *takes another pencil from* BILL'S *ear*) Thanks, man.

JOHN (*On* PHONE II): O.K. Shoot. (HE *points receiver at the audience. No shot.* HE *listens*)

PHONE II (*Mercury Message, in a "Thomas Mann voice"*): Gustave Aschenbach — or Von Aschenbach, as he had been known officially since his fiftieth birthday — had set out alone from his house in Prince Regent Street, Munich, for an extended walk.

JOHN *presses a number on the touchtone dial of* PHONE I.

PHONE II (*Thomas Mann voice, continued*): Aschenbach had sought the open soon after tea.

JOHN *presses three more numbers which play the opening phrase of Bach's "Toccata and Fugue in D Minor."*

PHONE II (*Thomas Mann voice, continued*): He was overwrought by a morning of hard nerve-taxing work . . .

A recording of the "Toccata and Fugue in D Minor" underscores the remaining portion of the quote from Mann's Death in Venice. JOHN, *in a "dumb show," appears to play it on the touchtone dials, expanding fingering to both* PHONES *as the fugue develops.*

PHONE II (*Thomas Mann voice, continued*): . . . work which had not ceased to exact his uttermost in the way of sustained concentration, conscientiousness, and tact; and after the noon meal he found himself powerless to check the onward sweep of the productive mechanism within him, that "motus animi continuus" in which, according to Cicero, eloquence resides. He had sought but not found relaxation in sleep — though the wear and tear upon his system had come to make a daily nap more and more imperative — and now undertook a walk, in the hope that air and exercise might bring him back refreshed to a good evening's work.

Bach pauses. JOHN *bows, acknowledging a tape of applause. Then Bach continues.*

PHONE II (*Thomas Mann voice, continued*): May had begun, and after weeks of cold and wet a mock summer had set in. The English Gardens, though in tenderest leaf, felt as sultry as in August and by the time he reached the North Cemetery he felt tired. But towards Aumeister the paths were solitary and still, and a storm was brewing over Föhring.

Music pauses.

JOHN (*On* PHONE II): Föhring?
PHONE II (*Mercury Message*): Ja, Föhring.

Bach and JOHN's *dumb show continues. The* TELEPHONES *rise, their poles elongating — the scene is lit as a holy tableau.* JOHN *climbs up his "cross of telephones" and hangs between them, still listening. Mercury Message's Thomas Mann voice continues throughout.*

PHONE II (*Thomas Mann voice*): A mortuary chapel in Byzantine style stood silent in the gleam of the ebbing day. Its facade was adorned with scriptural texts in gilded letters bearing upon the future life, such as: "They are entering into the House of the Lord" and "May the Light Everlasting shine upon them." Aschenbach let his mind's eye lose itself in these mystical formulas. He was brought back to reality by the sight of a figure standing in the portico above two apocalyptic beasts. The figure kindled his fantasy. He felt a kind of vaulting unrest. A youthful ardent thirst for distant scenes — a feeling so new, or at least so long ago outgrown and forgot, coming upon him with such suddenness and passion as to resemble a seizure.

The Bach and the Thomas Mann voice become deafening. JOHN *has a seizure.*

PHONE II (*Thomas Mann voice, continued*): He beheld a landscape, a tropical marshland full of islands, morasses, and alluvial channels . . .

JOHN hangs up PHONES. Silence. Short tableau. Then the TELEPHONES descend, bringing JOHN back to earth. JOHN dials PHONE I.

JOHN (*On PHONE I*): "Johns Anonymous." Well, look in the commercial listings. It's not in the commercial listings? I just got it from the commercial listings. Well, give me the supervisor. There's no supervisor? Well, give me my dime. What do you mean, "It's not my dime"! (*Hangs up*)

JOHN (*To BILL*): You got another dime?

BILL shakes his head.

JOHN (*To BILL, continued*): What do you mean, "You don't got another dime"!

Anxious pause until PHONE I rings.

JOHN (*Answering PHONE I*): "Johns Anonymous!" Whew . . . How'd you get my number? Oh . . . you called my Mother. Now she's giving out my number. I was picking up my messages. Sometimes you get long messages. Tom called. "*Tom*," man. "*Tom!*" Well, it's not hard to understand — the word is out, "I want to shoot in Venice"; he's pushing a script. Why should I mind? I don't write my scripts. I'm a *shooter* by profession — that's what I profess — I mean, I'm a "straight shooter." My problems lie in the area of projection. I remember, once, projecting "Imitation of Life" onto my dog. I made a mistake; it was a conceptual error. No, the problem was, this small domestic animal projected "Beauty and the Beast" right back on me. I was perceived. I perceived myself perceived. Right. I perceived I was not just some "Tom," "Dick" or "Harry." No, I was a "Jean." Right. I perceived that I, myself, was not a self-supporting system. I was a reactive system. I followed the action — all I needed was a little action. I followed other dogs; I panned around looking for little pussy cats; I zoomed in on a gerbil once because she thought I looked like Steve McQueen. Then I realized that my shooting was affected. I discovered that my shooting was affected shooting a long shot on 23rd Street. Formerly, when shooting, light entered my aperture through my lens and left an image right between my sprocket holes. But now, my light goes through my lens the other way and leaves my image on 23rd Street. (This was detailed in an article by Annette Michaelson called "The Greed Effect" — that's how it's referred to in the Industry today; in other circles it's called "The Miracle of 23rd Street" — it depends on your circle.) Well frankly, I had a creative crisis — three shots a day, then two (for a while there I was down to eighteen frames a week on Sunday afternoons). Then I cut out color. There I was down to black and white. I'd wake up in the morning with the shakes, my hair came out. I went on a bender; I shot two reels of "Todd AO" with quadraphonic sound. Afterwards, I was hospitalized. I emerged from the hospital a changed John. I was a *"Mark."* "You're a junkie, John," they told me, "you've got to go cold cock." I said, "I can't do it, Doc. I've found myself. I'm hooked on my reality. Now, I'm afraid to fade. My self is my vacation." What can I do? I go into myself. I become self involved. I try to be self effacing. But, that's self defeating. I indulge in self recrimination. But, all that does is make me more self centered. I long to be self transcending. But, this becomes too self deluding, which brings me to the brink of self destruction, which becomes a subject of self concern. Am I being self indulgent? Good. Good. Just checking. You got to help me, man, I'm going down the garden path — self assertion, then, self direction, then I get just plain old selfish — after which followeth self possession. I'm beside myself. That's the Pale Horse, man. I'm on the edge. I'm on the edge of being a *self made*, man.

The following Johns Anonymous monologue runs continuously. JOHN's *dialogue, first to* BILL *and then to the* OPERATORS *(local and transatlantic), is interjected into the pauses and over the lines of the monologue. The sequences begin at the points where they are inserted.*

PHONE I (*Johns Anonymous*): John, let me tell you the story of my life. My fucking did not start until after I was thirty-five, and a fairly successful career had been established. My success brought increased social activities, and I realized that many of my friends enjoyed a social fuck with no apparent harm to themselves or others. I disliked being different, so, ultimately, I began to join them occasionally.

JOHN (*To* BILL): You got about thirty-four dollars? I got to call Luxembourg.

BILL *shakes his head.*

JOHN *(To* BILL, *continued)*: Thanks anyway, my man, I'll call collect. You got a dime? Thanks, man.

PHONE I *(Johns Anonymous, continued)*: At first it was just that — an occasional fuck. Then I started looking forward to my weekend of golf and the nineteenth hole. Gradually the quantity increased; the occasions for fucking came more frequently — a hard day, worries and pressures, bad news, good news — there were more and more reasons to fuck. It was frightening. Fucking was being substituted for more and more of the things I really enjoyed doing. Golf, hunting, and fishing were now merely excuses to fuck excessively.

JOHN *(Dialing transatlantic operator on* PHONE II): Get me the Cable.

Dime comes back.

JOHN *(On* PHONE II, *continued)*: Thanks, man. The Transatlantic Cable. *(Pause)*: Informazione Luxembourg . . . Je voudrait . . . unt numer telefoon. Si. Lieba Stoed. Yah! "Es" "tay" "oh" "ooh" "day." Ja. O.K. Bon d'accord. Mit umlaut. Thanks, man.

PHONE I *(Johns Anonymous, continued)*: I made promises to myself, my family, my friends . . . and broke them. Short dry spells ended in heavy fucking. I tried to hide my fucking by going places where I was unlikely to see anyone I knew. Remorse was always with me. The next steps were closet fucking and excuses for trips in order to fuck without restraint — what it does to a person is apparent to everyone but the person involved.

JOHN *(On* PHONE II): Achtung! Hey ACHTUNG! Collectare.

PHONE I *(Johns Anonymous, continued)*: When it became noticeable to the point of comment, I devised ways of sneaking fucks on the side. Rehearsals became part of the pattern — stopping to fuck on the way to the place where I was planning to fuck — never having enough, always craving more; the obsession to fuck gradually dominated my entire life.

JOHN *(On* PHONE II): Allo! Prego! Pronto! Attenzione! What's happening! She won't accept? She rejects? Man, she don't understand, I live on the edge.

PHONE I *(Johns Anonymous, continued)*: I tried celibacy on numerous occasions but I always felt unhappy and abused. I tried psychiatry but, of course, I gave the psychiatrist no cooperation. I was living in constant fear that I would get caught fucking while driving a car, so I used taxis part of the time. Eventually, my entire personality changed to a cynical, arrogant, intolerant person, completely different from my normal self.

JOHN (*On* PHONE II): O.K., bill it to my home number. My home number — 911. It's an emergency.

PHONE I (*Johns Anonymous, continued*): I was full of self pity. I resented anyone and everyone who tried to get in my way. It seemed to me that my wife was becoming more intolerant and narrow-minded all the time; whenever we went out she appeared to go out of her way to keep me from having more than one fuck — she, of course, didn't realize how cunning a john can be. Our invitations became fewer and fewer; we had always encouraged our children to bring their friends home at any time, but, after a few experiences with a fucking father they eliminated home as a place to entertain their friends. I'll never know all the people I hurt, all the friends I abused, the humiliation of my family; we think we can fuck to excess without anyone knowing it — everybody knows it . . .

JOHN (*On* PHONE II): Hello. Lieba? Sorry. Where am I? I'm on the street. Where are you? On the bidet.

PHONE II *beeps.*

JOHN (*On* PHONE II, *continued*): Sorry. Well, the point is — Freddie Laker.

PHONE II *beeps again.*

JOHN (*On* PHONE II, *continued*): I thought you knew Freddie Laker. I thought I remembered you were intimate with Freddie Laker.

PHONE II *beeps again.*

JOHN (*On* PHONE II, *continued*): Well, the point is, "I've been cruising for years." The time has come to seek another mode of transportation.

PHONE II *beeps again.*

JOHN (*On* PHONE II, *continued*): Hang on a sec . . .
JOHN (*To* BILL): Did you hear a beep?

PHONE II *beeps.*

JOHN (*To* BILL, *continued*): Are they tracing my call?

PHONE II *beeps.*

JOHN (*On* PHONE II): I'll get back to you. (*Hangs up*)

*Police siren approaches. Stops. Red flashing light. White
spotlight on* BILL. HE *hides* JOHN.

N.Y.P.D. (*Over police bullhorn*): Hi . . . Have you seen some
dumb john about three foot two in a leather jacket with a
wooden head that just charged a call to Luxembourg to the
Fourth Precinct? . . . No, huh. Well, have you seen Carlo
Gambino? . . . No, huh. How about the Penguin? Lex
Luthor? "Bad . . . Bad . . . Leroy Brown — the Baddest Man in
the Whole Damn Town"? . . . No, huh. Well, man. Just keep
your eyes open!

Siren, departing, fades.

JOHN (*Dialing* PHONE I *and speaking before anyone is on the
line*): Mom . . . are you there? Where are you Mother? Are
you sitting by the fire? Mother . . . are you rocking? Are you
knitting? Are you whistling . . . Mother?

The call is picked up at the other end.

JOHN (*On* PHONE I, *continued*): Mummy, guess what I saw when
I looked in the mirror? Come on, guess. Mummy . . . don't
be a cunt. Guess how many. No, not six — eight. Right.
Eight. One here, three here, two here, and one short one
right over here. They kind of form a line. Right — a hair line.
It must be body chemistry. You stimulate my follicles.
Mother . . . you remember when I had a hairline. You used
to tell me stories about it. You remember — it was when we
lived in Venice; we used to sit by the pool and work on your
script, and you'd say, "Someday, when you're a pro, you'll
shoot it for me." You what? You dreamt I came on to you as
Saint Peter — the *rock* — and then you missed your period.

Mummy, you went through menopause in 1968. Summer of '68 . . . I brought you back to life . . . I see. And now, you'll do the same for me. No thanks. You know what I'm saying? I'm saying, "No thanks." Mother, if I'm born again — we're through. Don't do it Mummy . . .

JOHN (*To* BILL): She's going to do it.

JOHN (*On* PHONE I): Don't Mummy . . . Please! No, not again. Don't do it . . .

JOHN (*To* BILL): She's going to do it. She's doing it.

PHONE I *beeps.*

JOHN (*To* BILL, *continued*): She did it.

BILL (*To* JOHN): She did it?

JOHN (*To* BILL): She put me on hold.

JOHN *sits on curb in front of* TELEPHONES.

JOHN (*To* BILL, *continued*): I have to face facts. No, not those facts — broader facts. I have to face the fact that I'm an American Boy. I was a boy and his dog, and now I'm a boy and his Mother — that's a fact. I've been trying to produce myself for years — but I'm an American Boy — all I've become is a *consumer.* Now that the moment is at hand, I've got cold feet — all I want to do is consume myself. (*Pause*) In order to produce myself I've become a consumer. I'm going to have to change my life around. In order to consume myself — I'll become a *producer.* A producer . . . yeah . . . Well, I've started already — I've got an agent.

PHONE II *rings.* JOHN *answers.*

PHONE II (*Mercury Message*): John, your Dad called again. He's at another number.

JOHN (*On* PHONE II): Another number?

PHONE II (*Mercury Message*): Forest Lawn — extension 666.

JOHN (*On* PHONE II): The *beast.* I'll get right on it.

PHONE II (*Mercury Message*): John, don't sign anything.

JOHN (*On* PHONE II): Why not?

PHONE II (*Mercury Message*): Well . . . don't let this get around . . .

JOHN (*On* PHONE II): I don't . . .

PHONE II (*Mercury Message*): It won't be shot in Greece . . .

JOHN (*On* PHONE II): It won't?

PHONE II (*Mercury Message*): It's not that kind of shot.

JOHN (*On* PHONE II): It's not?

PHONE II (*Mercury Message*): It's a shot in the dark.

JOHN (*On* PHONE II): That's not my shot. (*Pause*) Put him on.

PHONE II (*Mercury Message*): John, if I put him on there's a surcharge.

JOHN (*To* BILL): Uh . . . you put him on.

BILL (*To* JOHN): I'll put him on.

JOHN (*On* PHONE II): He'll have to talk to my agent. Bill . . . Bill Morris . . . He's one of the biggest.

BILL (*On* PHONE II, *Bill Morris voice*): We don't want to shoot in Greece. We want to shoot in Venice — corner of Rose and Speedway — it's a very good location. No, we don't want Meryl Streep. We want "Mr. and Mrs. North and South America and all the ships at sea." You don't think so, huh. You don't think there's a buck in "Mr. and Mrs. North and South America and all the ships at sea"? Well, that's not what Danny Selznick thinks. You can fold that deal in with four phone calls. Listen Pop, you call Nat Feldman, Bernie Myerson; you call Salah Hassanian, Larry Lapidus, and you're home free. I said, "home free."

PHONE I *rings.* BILL *as Bill Morris answers.*

BILL (*On* PHONE I, *Bill Morris voice*): Hi. Tell me I'm brilliant — I'll tell you you're beautiful. Tell me again. Hey . . . you're beautiful . . . Ma, you don't get it — the producer mentality is dedicated to the "Art of Spiritual Advancement." My dog has grown a fingernail. On her paw, rear right. She's got four claws and one fingernail. Last night she had an avocado salad and a glass of Chablis. I just sprinkled a few Friskies on it instead of the croutons. That *is* the work! I am dedicated to the "Art of Spiritual Advancement." If I could subsidize a grasshopper into becoming a titwillow; if I could love enough — that bug would take one hop, catch a flying beetle, and just never come down. Ma, you've been saying I'm "God's gift" for forty years. Now, I believe it. I can't get off on anything except a miracle. For Christ's sake, I've experienced an epiphany. I took my vows in a Ukrainian delicatessen and right there I turned a Polish sausage into a boudin. I can *produce* reality.

Police siren approaches. Stops. Red flashing light. White spotlight on BILL. HE *hides* JOHN.

N.Y.P.D. (*Over police bullhorn*): Hi. Still got your eyes open? Good. Good. Just checking. Well, man, keep your ears open, too.

Siren, departing, then music from the street.

BILL Hey! Hey, would you mind turning that up a little?

Music up.

BILL (*Over music, continued*): Top of the world, Ma! So we made our first investment on a lease of a small second-run unit and started to get property around the key area of 59th Street and Third Avenue. The rest is history. (*Pause*) We don't want the *rest* of history. We want "that motus animi continuus in which," according to Cicero, "eloquence resides."

Music up. BILL *and* JOHN *dance.* BILL *bites* JOHN *on the neck.* JOHN *goes "dead" in his arms. Telephone lights change from white to red. Fog seeps in. A* BAT *flies around* PHONE I *and then perches on top of it.*

BILL (*Continued*): Hi, Sucker. What do you mean you're not home free? Well frankly, Pop, I'm shocked that you, of all people, are not home free; in fact, I'm shocked you're even home at all. Don't you usually wing it till sunrise before you crawl in and pull down the lid? I understand you filed an affidavit that I'm not an Equal Opportunity Employer. You stated that I discriminate against the dead. You work for me, Sucker. Don't you ever forget it! Hey, Pop, you're out for blood, aren't you? I understand, I really do — it's a hook. I'm telling you, "Eat those chocolate covered cherries." They're just as good. I left a whole box for you under the wolfbane. I said, "Eat those chocolate covered cherries!" "Eat those chocolate covered cherries. They're just as good! Good! Good!" Just *vamping* . . .

Music and lights start to fade.

BILL (*Continued*): You're suffering from claustrophobia? Pop . . . I'm sorry . . . You have to . . . what . . . you have to open the lid and look at the sky? That's dangerous. I mean — anybody just driving by with a stake and hammer . . . Your soul . . . ?

seeks the light . . . ? That's so weird, man. My body does. My body gets up at daybreak . . . sets the alarm for my soul at two a.m. We hardly have a thing in common anymore. I'm sorry too. There's nothing to say — you know what I'm saying? I'm just *vamping*. We're vamping, Sucker, you and me. We don't have a thing in common anymore.

The BAT *flies down and hovers by* BILL'S *ear.*

BILL (*Continued*): We do? (BILL *props* JOHN *up against* PHONE II) Uh huh . . . uh huh . . . uh huh . . . hey, do you mind if I bum one of those chocolate covered cherries? (BILL *magically materializes, unwraps and eats cherry*) Thanks, man. (BILL *leans against* PHONE I) Uh huh . . . well, why don't we have lunch sometime — a late lunch. Who would you like to eat? Well, it's business too — I want to incorporate. I want to incorporate in two states — "yours" and "mine." I want to work up a joint proposal. I need a little subsidy. Yeah, that's my point — supernatural subsidy. Well, you know the people, man . . . I mean . . . shit, man, you know Croesus. Right now I'm just a piece of chalk on the blackboard of myth. You got another chocolate covered cherry? (*Again* BILL *magically materializes, unwraps and eats cherry*) Thanks, man. Well, I was going to wait to get into this over lunch, but, if you've got a minute, I could pitch it to you. All I want is a development deal. Uh huh . . . and pursuant to our previous discussion, Pop, I want to shoot in Venice. *PLEASE*. Thanks, man. I want to shoot you sitting in the fog, on a bench, on a beach in Venice. We'll use fast film 'cause there's not much light. There's not much color. I'm on your lap. (BILL *sits on the curb*) I'm down inside your overcoat like a kangaroo in a pocket. Well, that's my shot. Yeah, that's my point — it's a *lap* dissolve. You got another cherry? (*Again* BILL *magically materializes, unwraps and eats cherry*) Thanks, man. I want your shoes off, and your feet in the sand, and your eyes on the water, and your hair in the fog. You know, it's Venice before the mist burns off — it's *vamping* weather. And I say to you, Pop, "How do you do?" How does a *doer* do . . . or die . . . ? And you say, "*You vait for de sun, son, like any udder sucker.*" Now . . . dissolve to the sun.

The sun appears in the night sky over the street. BILL *takes his jacket and shirt off.*

BILL (*Continued*): The sun comes right down Pico Boulevard beating every yellow light. The *son* is looking for you. (*Music, lights and effects fade*) I want to die in my father's arms looking at the sea. Repeat after me . . .

BILL *sings to the tune of "Row, Row, Row Your Boat." The voice of a child joins the round faintly.*

BILL (*Continued*):
I want to die in my father's arms
   Looking at the sea.
I want to die in my father's arms.
   Repeat after me . . .

Round repeats. Music, lights and effects out. Round breaks off. The BAT *flaps its wings, still hovering at* BILL'S *ear.*

BILL (*Continued*): Yeah . . . well, just bring along one of your standard contracts. Yeah . . . yeah, I'll sign in blood.

VAMPIRE BAT *flies off.*

BILL (*Aside, continued*): Jesus Christ . . . what a primitive . . . (BILL *calls after the departing* BAT *and the "departed" music*) Thanks, man . . .

END

IV

28. I was told that cells are replaced every seven years; that the cells that wrote *Sister Suzie Cinema* were not the cells that wrote *Red Beads* , unless from the point of view of one toward the other, or the other toward the one—I was *acting*.

29. *"So you want to be an actress!"* This is known as *Boleslavski's camp* and there are various versions. If you've put the right name by the right *camp* your matching quiz should read like this:

Stand on your head	Grotowski
Do what I tell you	Reinhardt
Get a little distance	Brecht
Dream	Richardson
Feel now, show later	Stanislavski
Be cruel	Artaud
Don't be cruel, be a flower	Zeami
Take it off	Judith and Julian
Put it on	R. Foreman
Acting is semiotics	Del Sarte
Acting is biological mechanics	Meyerhold
I am the truth	Strasberg
No! I am the truth	Bobby Lewis

30. These *camps* pretend to be scientific. It follows, then, that poetry is theatrical pork, and science must be kosher.

31. Descartes is the culprit. All is mathematics, even art. Scientific materialism turns *right* into particle physics while turning *left* into Brecht. And Stanislavski's is a nice equation too. Acting equals Freud times Pavlov not so squared.

32.   Actors can be their own *rats* and *Skinners* too. Actors are able to be other than they are by simulating the conditions of otherness and responding thereto. Actions, objectives, sense memories are a great gong show. Each salivation required by the script has its own bell. Acting is the electrochemical response which triggers muscles to form expressions, gestures, postures — a semiotic vocabulary that excites our empathy or antipathy according to scientific laws no different for us than for the Stickleback. Motivational acting is the name of a biological program.

33.   *Personalization* — an idea credited to Stanislavski, has been bandied about psychologically by Strasberg and esoterically by Grotowski. Roughly speaking, character and emotion are represented by recreating and remixing parts of yourself (your *self* being a Proustian entity of selves piled upon one another in remembered time). Characterization is persona recombinant. Under sexual tension, mix parts of yourself, and like the DNA in meiosis, out comes the illusion of a new human being. Science — love it or leave it.

34.   If you want to leave it, you can always account for a great performance as voodoo. You can account for acting by saying that if you pray to the Lua, and if the drums speak the right language, the God understands and comes down and rides. You are the horse of God. You are mounted. You dance. A horse of God dances. And where you will be ridden by God, called here Inspiration, no one knows. Sometimes it's dangerous.

35.   Art, the gift, is sometimes dangerous but even so, I wouldn't put Descartes before de horse.

36.   The Reverend Earl E. Miller, speaking at Yale Drama School, said that Pentacostal preaching was acting for God. Is writing, acting for the heroes? A characterization of mind costumed in ego? What ghostly peers are expected to applaud the performance on the page? I think a writer's like a typecast actor who outgrows the role. Unable to bring off the old "strut and fret" he takes a deep breath and tries a new one. It's the cells that die and the tone of voice goes with them. You try to keep faith in the muse. But always between the Crucifixion and the Resurrection there are a few tense days.

The 1982 work-in-progress production of *Red Beads* at the Empty Space in Seattle with Marjorie Nelson, Susan Heldfond, Clare Dewey and Frank Corrado.

Red Beads

Red Beads *opened as a work-in-progress on February 3, 1982, at the Empty Space in Seattle. It was directed by Lee Breuer, with music by William Spencer, choreography by Susan Heldfond and design by Thom Cathcart. The Father was played by Frank Corrado, the Mother by Susan Heldfond, the Daughter was Clare Dewey and the Narrator, Marjorie Nelson.* Red Beads *was adapted from a story by Polina Klimouitskaya.*

A house under a spell. A carpet of leaves. The wind blows. Exterior becomes interior. Leaves cover the floor, the furniture, they become a quilt on a child's bed, a ghostly love seat. Half buried in them, a stuffed cat and a dog and a candle in a candlestick, a toy bird and a picture book. Interior becomes exterior. Rakes like country brooms, the haunted moonlight. In a tale told by witches in a coven, a fated passion is replayed each Hallowe'en in the manner of a dream.

Morning

Enter the FATHER in a robe
with a copper tray, toast,
milk and jam:

THREE days before she was thirteen
The child came down to breakfast
Combed and clean, to find her father

Going upstairs with a copper tray.

Enter the DAUGHTER and
sees that:

On the tray was thin toast with the
Crust trimmed off, strawberry jam

And a bowl of milk.

FATHER:

                              Mother is pale

DAUGHTER:

Her father said. He knocked
On the bedroom door as soft as silk

The FATHER exits

The DAUGHTER sings:

                    Mother ate the strawberry jam
                    Right out of the spoon, and drank
                    The milk and left the toast

                    How pale she was with strawberry
                    Mouth and milk skin, pale as a ghost

and after singing, says:

Around her neck were red beads

Keep your promise, Daddy dear.
When I'm thirteen the thirteen beads
Are mine to wear . . .

Night

The DAUGHTER lights her
candle

Enter the FATHER, disturbed
and disheveled. He drinks
whiskey from a flask:

That night in her room she said
Her prayers by the light of a candle
Dipped in bay.

DAUGHTER: Said her father as he
                       Tucked her in,

FATHER: For what did you pray?

DAUGHTER: I prayed for my dog and my cat
                       And my bird. I prayed for my red beads

                       Ten plus three.

FATHER: Did you pray for your
                       Soul!

DAUGHTER: No, I forgot. Will you punish me?

MOTHER: He kissed her hard and closed the door

                       And the wind came up out of the floor

**The FATHER exits, drunk,
having covered the daughter
in leaves**

**MOTHER and DAUGHTER sing
a round. They rake leaves in
a trance:**

                              Birthdays, birthdays
                                Flowers and weeds
                              Wind and lightning
                                Thirteen beads

FATHER: The words of the wind in her Mother's
                       Voice came through the window into her ear

**He alternates with the
MOTHER singing the round**

MOTHER: Are you brave, child? Come outside. I have
                       Your birthday present here.

FATHER: She heard
                       Red beads falling, tinkling on the lawn

                       Her dog leapt through the window
                       Like an angel at a ghost. She
                       Heard him howl like the wind

                       Or was the wind like a howling dog?

RED BEADS

DAUGHTER:	Daddy, save me, please,
MOTHER:	she cried And pulled the covers over her head

And hid her face till the wind
Was mute and the beads were still
And her dog was dead . . .

MOTHER, FATHER and
DAUGHTER sit on the love
seat and read from a picture
book:

TWO days before she was thirteen
The child came down to breakfast
Dressed in green, to find her father

Going upstairs with a silver tray.
On the tray were tiny cakes and
Cherry preserves and a pot of tea

"Mother is pale," her father said.
"But Father, you are paler . . .
He put the tray down by the door

The DAUGHTER slips from
their arms and rolls
dreaming in the leaves:

And took her hand and held it close
First to his heart, then to
His lips, then to his forehead

The reading continues till
the MOTHER sings:

Birthdays, birthdays
Flowers and weeds
Wind and lightning
Thirteen beads

The DAUGHTER, dreaming:

Is that my mother singing, Father

Back behind the door?

The MOTHER, reading:

                     He hurried in

The FATHER, reading:

She ran away and hid all day
In the autumn field of harvest hay

MOTHER and FATHER now continue as a chorus:	She watched from the field and She watched from the hill and she Watched from the bank of the stream
The DAUGHTER in the leaves, sleepwalking, pantomimes the reading in a dumbshow:	All day long the house was still Not a puff of smoke, not one Leaf fell. And the sun went down As if under a spell. And the beetles Dreamed.
DAUGHTER, sleepwalking:	Daddy, come and find me I have your breakfast in a bowl A fig, a pear, a lock of my hair Tonight I'll pray to save my soul! Daddy! Come and help me. Daddy! Help me bury my dog.
The FATHER joins the DAUGHTER in her pantomime:	He came At once with pick and spade.
The DAUGHTER, still dreaming:	Suddenly She was afraid. He spoke to her
FATHER and DAUGHTER together:	You take the tongue and I the tail We'll throw her into the rocky shale and Cover her with mud. And mark her grave With a drop of blood. With a bead!
DAUGHTER, dreaming:	All this my Daddy strangely said and Quickly turned,
FATHER:	Now come to bed.

The FATHER carries the
DAUGHTER in his arms and
sings:

That night in her room she could not
Pray. She could not speak or
Even lay her head upon the pillow

It was wet with fever sweat
"Can't sleep. Won't sleep. I'll
Bite my tongue. I'll pinch my feet."

FATHER and sleepwalking
DAUGHTER dance:

Her cat jumped down with a tiny moan
Her bird rocked on its perch without
A sound. Then, like the shiver of an

Eyelash of a girl who starts to cry
Rain dropped out of a shivering sky
Her mother spoke again that night

MOTHER and FATHER, singing
a duet:

Come down to the basement, dear
I have a present for you here to
Celebrate your thirteenth year.

MOTHER, FATHER and
DAUGHTER, singing a trio:

She heard a cry at the cellar
Door. And a sound like
Marbles over the floor. Like

Rats running up the wall. The
Child could not see at all.
Morning . . . . . . They found

In a cellar stall, her kitten
Curled into a ball. And small
Red marks where it was bitten

Morning

Playthings spread for a play
picnic. The FATHER and
DAUGHTER in the leaves play
a "Paddycake" clapping
game:

Come to breakfast, father. Sleepy
Head! The sun is high. There's cream
In the pitcher and bread in the stove

And speckled egg pie and flowers
On the table set for two — just me and
You.

The DAUGHTER **breaks off:**   Last night I had a fever.

FATHER: Daughter, Mother's so pale I dare not
Leave her. Bring plum jam on a golden
Tray and coffee, black, and stay away

The FATHER **exits**

The MOTHER **and** FATHER, **in
the love seat, sing:**   *The child knocked at the bedroom door*

The DAUGHTER **enters
enraged. Speaking:**   Mother and Father, it's a shame to treat
A daughter so who's not to blame

Who'll be thirteen on Hallowe'en. I am
A woman, Mother, just like you I want
My Daddy! I want my due — a house

Of joy and end to sorrow.

FATHER, **speaking:**   Her mother
Said,

MOTHER, **singing:**   *Not till tomorrow!*

DAUGHTER, **speaking:**   Give me

My red beads! Mother!

MOTHER, **singing:**   *Not till*

Tomorrow!

Then speaking: They lay there both so pale
So pale from tip of toe to top of head
"Father," she said. "My cat is dead!"

The DAUGHTER, amid
showers of whirling leaves,
buries her kitten. The
FATHER calls:

She buried her kitten in the ground
And ran so far she couldn't
Be found. Her father called all day

In the woods he'd call three times and
Stop to listen. Three times he'd call
And stop to sigh. Each time he called

She started to cry.

DAUGHTER:

                  I'll never
Go back home,

MOTHER:

                      she thought. But deep
Inside her thinking was the deeper

Thing she sought.

DAUGHTER:

                  I'll go back
One more time. At midnight
The red beads will be mine. . . .

The DAUGHTER sings:

THE NIGHT before she was thirteen
No one came. She lay upon
Her back unkissed. How cold

Was her bed where once a dog
Had slept and where a cat had kept
A green-eyed vigil by her head

In the stillness of the night her
Father locks his bedroom door. She
Hears his footsteps to the bed

Make ripples on the floor. The
Night. A black pond. Each sound
Falls in like a stone. "He's afraid

To leave my mother. I'm afraid
To be alone." The sky outside her
Window. Was it blackest night?

Or brightest day? Or was it
Lightning without thunder? My God!
It's twelve! She had forgot to pray!

The MOTHER sings:

Come to the attic, Daughter. It's the
Door at the top of the stairs. If you
Want the red beads that Mother wears!

**Choral recitative, MOTHER
and DAUGHTER. They
perform the actions
described:**

In the attic, in the shadow, in
The corner of her eye waited
Her mother, pale as morning clouds

Hair white as winter morning sky

MOTHER alone:

O daughter,

MOTHER and DAUGHTER:

said the mother

MOTHER alone:

Does it have to end this way?

Is passion's jewel for one to lose
And one to gain upon a given day?

DAUGHTER alone:

O mother,

MOTHER and DAUGHTER:

said the daughter

DAUGHTER alone:

I did not make the rules
I made not women live for love
Nor made I men all fools

MOTHER and DAUGHTER:

Then she unclasped her mother's necklace
Never once did their eyes meet
And held it to her own white skin

Red beads like drops of blood
Upon a sheet.

MOTHER alone:	Count them, daughter Thirteen. Every bead is there!
MOTHER and DAUGHTER:	She wound them 'round the girlish Throat and twisted! Whistling Through the air the bird careened From room to room to find the father
DAUGHTER alone:	Quick! Come quick!
MOTHER alone:	For it's your Daughter's doom!
MOTHER and DAUGHTER:	The mother gasped
MOTHER alone:	Here will begin my second life I'll live again in you. Woman's Born in blood. The child must First go to her grave. You'll die And I'll become the child again While you become love's slave.
DAUGHTER alone:	Daddy! Save me!
MOTHER and DAUGHTER:	cried the daughter Necklace 'round her throat. But when He came a pale young girl sat motionless Remote.
DAUGHTER alone:	Save me, Daddy. Save me
FATHER alone, entering:	How her voice had changed and how her Eyes were burning and her heart deranged
The FATHER, recitative over music:	Her father said, "You know the truth The beads are yours. She was a witch And I in thrall. Your mother's lost We'll look for her. You know the truth Once and for all. You and I dear Daughter, we will hold each other

By the hand and vow a vow of fealty
To the rightful lady of the land."

FATHER, MOTHER and
DAUGHTER sing:

All
Hallow's Eve they search, the pair, the

Father dark, the daughter fair. "Mother
Is lost. Search low and high." But they
Never find her. The truth was a lie

END

V

37.   There is no such thing as a director. There is only this thing of a *t'ing*. When you leave out the *h* you leave out one hemisphere, two worlds, and six continents because da Caribbean *t'ing*—in fact, any *t'ing* any place you find it—is really the *African t'ing* on a world cruise.

38.   Have you ever met a director with anything to say? I doubt it. Have you met a typist with something to write about? There is no such thing as a director because directing, like typing, is a skill. Who you probably have met, in the theatre or on the set, is some creative individual, say, a poet (Brecht) or an actor (Stanislavski) or a painter (Wilson) with a tangential skill. You may have even met a producer. The art of producing is to work with certain materials called *realities*—real money, real people, real estate. It is a curious, difficult, and limited medium that cannot rest with truth and beauty. It can only succeed with success.

39.   But your *t'ing* is not your skill. It is not even your art. Is it your song? Yes and no. Your sex? Is that the little *t'ing* itself? Your style, your totem, your phenomenological fingerprint? (If it is, you better figure out another way to say it or it gets to be another thing.) *T'ing* is your piece of the big picture puzzle given to you alone to play with for a lifetime. *T'ing* is soul.

40.   Poets of the oral tradition are pulled by the tongue's music away from the printed page. A writer with a directing flair is pulled into a love affair with *image*. In Japanese, writing and painting are the same word. Illustrated scrolls and Egyptian tombs and Gothic windows, like the comics and the movies, tell stories. We word pictographers live in a dream. We dream we are Fellinis trailing clouds of *lire*. In cruel reality we are cutters and splicers on an imagery dole; we are the mixers who've never mixed their rock and roll.

41.   When my choices were made for me, no movements were moving, there were no drafts to dodge or spiritual awakenings to set the alarm for, no drugs or wars to O.D. on. The most dramatic way out was to total your car. Failing death by Rocket 88, "sensibilities" were hauled into court and sentenced to a "life" of wearing black turtleneck sweaters and drinking espresso coffee on Filbert and Grant.

42.   At UCLA in the fifties there was no way out but art, and art was celluloid. A way with words never took the form of the sentence, a way with the drama, never an act or a scene. Cut-up and mix-down were the iambs and trochees of the Burbank muse.

43.   Here is the cut-up and mix-down recipe for *Hajj*. Take two poems in two styles (*Lies!* after *Sister Suzie Cinema* and *Hajj* after *Red Beads*). Cut and mix. Take two different first persons of two different sexes, two voices, two attitudes, two debts, two deaths. Cut and mix. Take two languages (verbal, the text, and visual, Craig Jones's video and Julie Archer's installation). Cut, mix and prepare over a flame. For the dialectics, Ruth Maleczech's performance is the synthesizing flame.

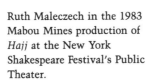

Ruth Maleczech in the 1983
Mabou Mines production of
Hajj at the New York
Shakespeare Festival's Public
Theater.

Hajj

Hajj *premiered in May 1983 at the New York Shakespeare Festival's Public Theater and is now in the repertoire of Mabou Mines. A collaborative work, it combined Lee Breuer's poetry and direction with the performance of Ruth Maleczech, the videography and live mix of Craig Jones and an installation designed and constructed by Julie Archer.*

Music was composed, programmed and performed by Chris Abajian; makeup and mask were designed and constructed by Linda Hartinian; live cameras were operated by Stephanie Rudolph, David Hardy and Ghretta Hynd; the engineer was J.T. Moore. Phil Schenk played the role of the grown-up on videotape, and Lute Ramblin' the role of the child. Hajj *was commissioned by Joseph Papp and the New York Shakespeare Festival.*

Lights discover the PERFORMER *seated, back to audience, before a low makeup table with a large triptych mirror that shows her triple reflection to the audience — tile surface, Arabic motifs, a clutter of toiletries and makeup paraphernalia. She has previously put up her hair, blocked out her eyebrows and put on alcohol. Now she attaches an elastic headband and applies the six tapes requisite for an onstage face-lift. Then she applies liquid base. Her voice is amplified.*

Three closeups of the PERFORMER *appear in the three planes of the triptych mirror. The effect is achieved by the placement of color video monitors behind one-way mirrors connected to three cameras in a reverse studio configuration — three closed-circuit systems functioning simultaneously.* PERFORMER *speaks simultaneously to herself and to her reflections.*

    I have
    Nothing to
    Hide . . .

SHE *appears to blow out the images as if they were candles and repeats*

    I have
    Nothing to
    Hide . . .

while reaching for eyeliner, which is in a set of nine colors mounted in a plastic display case. It resembles an enlarged electronic calculator or adding machine. The eyeliners are in actuality buttons that activate phrases of computer-programmed music that allude to electronic calculating machines. The music plays. A camera closeups a price tag on a hairdryer reading "$99.98." The PERFORMER *reads*

    . . . ninety
    Nine, ninety
    Eight

PERFORMER, *utilizing hairdryer to dry makeup base, shown in close shot, says*

    I can take
    Anything . . .

SHE *activates "eyeliner" computer—music pours forth.* SHE *continues*

> . . . three
> Bills a week
> Less the Social
> Security

More "cash register" music. SHE *sings*

> The man that
> I marry
> Will come cash
> And carry . . .

"Cash register" bells with a conga beat

> I hear
> My music
> Playing . . .

A camera begins a very slow, sensuous pan in extreme closeup of all the bells and bottles on the table that continues throughout the following. Sonorous silvery bells play.

> . . . thirty
> Pieces of silver

The PERFORMER *applies, between each line, various colors of liner and rouge. Each time* SHE *touches a color of her "palette," the color acts as a computer button and music pours forth.*

> I'll pay you
> Tomorrow . . .

A closeup of a kleenex—on it is written "$5.09."

> . . . @
> Five O nine

SHE *takes the kleenex from the box, uses it, crumples, tosses.*

> I'll pay you
> The day after
> Tomorrow . . .

Another closeup of kleenex — on it written "$7.42."

    . . . @
Six forty-two

SHE *takes from box, uses, crumples, tosses.*

    I'll pay you
Half, (that's forty
By Friday), then
If I can . . .

Closeup of kleenex with words "post date."

    . . . post
Date a check
I'll drop the
Rest off Monday
Before seven . . .

Music — eight bells. SHE *corrects herself*

Eight . . .

Music — ten bells. The extreme closeup camera pan is now showing the tiny bells scattered around the table that produce the bell sounds.

Ten . . .

Twelve bells

    I know! You
Need it! Now
Would I try to
Rip you off? Twelve . . .

Thirty quick bells.

    Thirty. By Friday
And the rest by the
First . . .

Bells play — first half of Big Ben motif.

. . . Even . . .

Second half of Big Ben motif.

. . . Steven

Bells play first half of Mendelssohn's "Wedding March" motif.
SHE *says to her reflection*

I love you . . .

Second half of "Wedding March" motif.

I now pronounce you a
Pound of flesh @ two
Nineteen a pound

*The extreme closeup pan of the objects on the table comes to
rest on a blonde wig as for a child. The* PERFORMER's *hand
caresses it on camera in the manner of a filmic insert.* SHE *says*

I love you
Daddy . . .

*A close shot of the body of a sleeping child about eight years
old, the camera panning the full length of the body. The image
floats across all three mirror/monitors like a dream or mem-
ory — sound of wind and distant sheep bleating. The* PER-
FORMER's *memories are shown, as here, by prerecorded imagery
on tape that is patched into the closed-circuit systems at the
appropriate times. The live, closed-circuit camera work then
stands for her mentation and associations in the present, as
distinct from the prerecorded, taped sequences, which eluci-
date her memories and daydreams from the past. Over the im-
age of the child,* SHE *says*

The day before yesterday
The truth put me to sleep
A hailstorm on my fingers
Did not wake me, nor
A light shining in my eye

A distant phrase of Al Adan Al Charhi, *the Arabic call to prayer,
is heard.*

The prophet of loss sang
Too faintly. I heard not
Scripture

Closeups of the PERFORMER — *profile, then from the reverse pro-*
file — pan across the mirrors. SHE *is putting on mascara.*

The problem is cash
   That's a lie
The problem is cash flow
   That's a lie
The problem is flow
   Don't you know

Closeup pans in opposite direction. SHE *puts on lipstick.*

Lies! A study in cost
Accounting. Lies!
A chronicle of expenditures
Lies! All lies! All. . .

Video image of PERFORMER's *face, tightly cropped, in a hand*
mirror.

My life
Sucks . . .

SHE *lights a cigarette.*

   . . . @ big
Bucks

Blows out image. Turns downstage and puffs.

You
Turn me on . . .

Activates computer music which alludes to a telephone
ringing.

   . . . @
Two bits over
Drawn

Ringing continues.

I'll get back
To you:

Continues.

. . . time
And charges

Continues.

I'm coming: . . .

SHE *blows smoke. Amplified, the music resembles a jet plane.*

. . . L Ten
Eleven.

Cameras zoom over the table.

I'm going. . .

The image resembles an aerial view.

. . . @ Seven
Forty-Seven

PERFORMER *reclines with her head propped against the table, smoking the cigarette. Reverse-angle closeups of her on mirror monitors.*

I have a spiritual life
Package includes . . .

A single bell tone introduces each.

. . . food, shelter,
Pediatrician, tuition,
Orthodontist, summer camp,

Side cameras' closeups slowly recede.

Loan, lawyer, bail, shrink,
Pension and ascension. Gravestone

Inscribed *Here Lies a Spiritual Life* @
One hundred and twenty-four
Thousand eight hundred forty twenty-two
(None of this is tax-deductible at present
But there's a bill pending . . .)

As SHE *smokes, her face is replaced by closeups of the cigarette smoke on the mirror/video screens.*

There is a womb of air
    Between my feet and the floor
There is a womb of silence
    Between my voice and your ear
There is a womb of lies
    Between my mind and life
            I'm a pea
            In a shell game
            Don't bet on me
            Five'll get you three

Here begins a long memory sequence on videotape, utilizing various combinations of the mirror/video screens. We see mysterious and lyric views of an old World War II Army truck, still and in motion — on roads and in an open field — snow on the ground. Once, we see a close shot of a hunting rifle on the truck seat and the PERFORMER *lying by it superimposed.* SHE *reaches for the gun. Suddenly, the sound of thunder. The truck and its occupants — the* PERFORMER *as a* CHILD, *and an adult — perhaps her father — are traveling. The journey has spiritual overtones, a pilgrimage of sorts. The* CHILD, *riding, speaks to the camera in closeup.*

I sing of you, Alex, who I killed (of course I did)
And thank you, dear . . .

The PERFORMER *joins the* CHILD, *lips synching.*

. . . for every fantasy I reaped
And curse you, cunt
        I owe you money

You've been dead for half my life. You are
My half life, love; you date my art

The CHILD's *voice drops out, leaving the* PERFORMER's *voice*
post-synchronizing the image of the CHILD. SHE *is now dressed*
identically to, and made up to resemble, the CHILD *in the truck.*
An old patchwork quilt around her shoulders, blonde wig, face-
lift with youthful-seeming base and coloration, the same or-
ange bandana the CHILD *wears in the image.* HER *voice seeks to*
recreate the CHILD's *phrasing.*

 I see my art in the green glow of radium
 Always less by half; I see this game
 As cute as archaeology
    I'm gonna pay you

 Baby, watch me dig you up
 And stuff it up your anus magnus
 Watch me write this
    I sing of you

Over an image of the truck receding into the twilight — country
desolate, winter road — the PERFORMER's *face (live, closed-cir-*
cuit) is superimposed on the prerecorded sky. SHE *speaks, less*
now in the CHILD's *phrasing.*

   Once
 Once a life wallpaper smokes
 Yellow leaf clusters flare, fall, flake away
 Under my bare, bathed footprints. Once
 Once a life the clock, the demon reads aloud
 The writing on the other wall
    A call to pilgrimage

Other images of the truck appear simultaneously, traveling
other roads.

 Lo and behold we're on our way (follow the bouncing ball)
 The sun looks like a melted Deutschmark; it acetylenes
 The scenery — roads, rivers, rocks like crap on the
    Ten below snow

 I think of your ribs and your life in my mind

The mirrors go black. Then, headlamps shine through the two side mirrors, making them appear like headlamps of the truck, and the mirrors like windshields.

The sun goes out *ssst* like a match into a wave
We're on our way to Cheat's Bay *ssst* . . .

Headlamps go out.

> . . . lights out
> Let's drive in darkness

The mirror/screens show views from inside the speeding truck — left and right closeups of the rearview mirrors showing winter trees, streams and mountains speeding by; center, the winding road over the hood. The soundtrack — a Dervish chant, The Mawlid-Invocation of the Divine Name, *over the truck motor. The head of the* PERFORMER *making a sign of the devil with her fingers is superimposed over the windshield — the image is of the* CHILD *riding in the truck.* SHE *growls in a devil's voice.*

Ready or not, Al, here I come with cash
My check's no good, dead man
I come to sodomize you with a
> Roll of Jacksons

The PERFORMER *dances against the images of the speeding truck — speeding forward and backward, by rearview mirror reflection — at the same time.* SHE *spins as a Dervish and simultaneously, mimetically drives the truck like a child playing with a steering wheel. Vocally,* SHE *roars as the motor which, electronically altered, appears to become a blood-curdling scream. The onrushing truck swerves off the road and careens into the mouth of a mountain cave like the opening of an Egyptian tomb. And the screens go black. The sound of a deluge of rain, an echoing gunshot — echoing like the thunder. The image of rain splattering over a rock. In the rock, the* PERFORMER'*s face superimposed — weeping.* SHE *mourns*

If I sell this Alexander I will move your bones to Persia
Want to bet me, conquerer of Asia? Put your money
> Where your mouth was

*In the center of the triptych a memory image: the truck in a
blizzard of snow. The* CHILD, *under the quilt, struggling home to
an old weathered farm house. Inside, the* CHILD *held in the*
FATHER's *arms, being rocked to sleep, speaks as if in a dream.*

    If only I can talk to you, Ali
        lovingly

The PERFORMER, *on closed-circuit in the side mirror/screens,
looking like the* CHILD, *appears to hold herself in her own arms
in the same position. They continue speaking together.*

    Here in the moon-blanched kitchen of my dreaming
    Powder snow blowing
        In a genie gust

    Or in the bathtub of my memory lit by nostalgia's candles
    Shadows of cats on the shadowy walls chasing shadows of
        Mice on the ceiling

    If I can talk to you with a tongue fresh licked
    By a tongue fresh licked I will be better
    Every time a little better
        Bled of pride

A blackout — all video goes dead.

        Alex
    You go dead on me.

The PERFORMER *now speaks without amplification and un-
enhanced by video.* SHE *changes her makeup, wig, costume and
character to that of a woman, half martyr, half whore—
strangely like the* CHILD *decayed.* SHE *completes her makeup
with the insertion of three bejeweled teeth fitting over her own.*

        You are the one
    I can't pay off; I can't put off your bill until
    The day after tomorrow when I score
    (I'll score for more the day I eulogize my owing)
    Unhappily, you're through. There's just
    no coming through for you
        (You done me see I ain't a good guy)

I can't suck my absolution from your collarbone
  And you can't cry

  Love is money Alex; money, love
  That's all ye need to know
    The terms

  I owe you forty dollars
  Alexander of the earth
      Now let's do business

I can't talk to you. I talk to money
Money knows me; we make deals

  Throw me a line

I'll write it on you, Alex, with my fingernail
  Below your spine

  Once you die you live forever
  Once you've lived you're good as gone
  One's the billing, one's the fee
  Up your black bone, baby
      Cash me in secrecy

SHE *takes a flashlight in hand and speaks to men in the au-*
dience, one by one, searching out the darkened faces, holding
and releasing them with the flashlight beam.

How strange the night, Alexis, sleeping with you
In the Fourteenth Arrondissement, in the brass bed
(Fuck, the mummy bag on the echo stone in
Agamemnon's tomb — it was raining)
O non dimenticare, Alex. Sleeping with you
On the Via Fiorello under the Lambrettas
(Fuck, on the train to you, you beautiful Champagne,
Urbana). In the canyon (fuck, Coldwater Canyon)
In the hottub, under the water, in front of the fan
(Fuck, fire). On the roof (the floor) of west six seven
Push B three (fuck, east B at three push C on four)
  Behind a window on the snowy sky
  Into which so many blackbirds fly

  ALEX!

Bells play a little lullaby. SHE *sings*

> *I hear my music playing*
> *I hear all my loves*
> *They're singing, listen, Alex*
> *I hear what I'm saying, listen*
> *All the prayer bells stopped*
> > *Ringing*

SHE *dances. The bottles and bells syncopate like a belly dance.*
SHE *holds the flashlight in her crotch and seduces the audience*
with its beam.

> Strange the night, Alexis, sleeping with you . . .
> > *Fuck . . . you . . .*
> On the set of Hotel Universe. The keys
> To Hotel Universe are in my pocket
> Under the mat at the desk in an envelope
> By the flowerpot second from left . . . *fuck*
> > *Right . . . fuck . . . left*

> The keys to Hotel Universe on key rings with
> Initials *A B C D E F G*
> > *H I J K L M N Ohh . . .*

> > *I hear my music playing*
> On the keys to Hotel Universe. The key rings
> *1 2 3-4 5 6 7   8 9 0-1 2 3 4* Hello . . .

The face of an old man appears in the center video. The image
pans from one old man's face to another echoing the manner in
which SHE *lit faces in the audience.*

> > I hear you
> You're the one that rings a little dead
> The gray eye looking inward, blue eye
> Darting from side to side. An ear *tick tick tick*
> To the geiger counter of obsession, ear
> To decay — the half life that fits the half life
> > Me half you

The PERFORMER*'s face in color, superimposed over the black-*
and-white portraits of the old men, appears to search them out
while speaking. Her hand in closeup on the side mirror/screens
clicks keys like zil *to the continuing rhythm.*

Your face appears in other faces
Eyes swim up in other eyes. Your touch
Touches me, it's other fingers. Your death dies
    Tingaling in everything

The PERFORMER's *face in color comes to rest, precisely superimposed over the face of Alex in the black-and-white photograph. He appears to come alive as her lips move over his.* SHE *says*

Right here . . . I write. Here I come, back
In love with you again . . . again. Alexandra
Read my writing. Open your eyes Janus-headed
Ghost of girl called fear of life and fear
    Of life to come

Closed-circuit closeup pans of the PERFORMER *left and right mirror/screen and super closeup of her mouth — jeweled teeth flashing — center.*

    Love is money Alex; money, love
    And that's not all ye need to know
    Ye need to know that hate is owing

Music of the bells and bottles distorted, strange, echo. Makeup table glows — infernal light, smoke. Blinding herself with the flashlight, SHE *searches for and finds the bier (the table) and mounts it.*

    Speculation
That I find your grave by matchlight
In the winter. Fog lights on the river ice
I can't believe my eyes; the glow of amber
Glow of fire flowing underneath. How deep we are
    Dear gentleman

    My soul smokes as I live and breathe
    My tongue is orange; my weapon is green
    My name is debtor — the unforgiven
    My vision is a debtor's prison

On video, the flashlight picks out her black dressing gown thrown on the corner of the makeup table. SHE *lifts it. Under it, appearing on all three monitors, is a lifelike latex mask of Alex Lujak, lying on the dark background of the tiled surface like a death mask.* SHE *sits down on the table and prepares to put the mask on. As* SHE *speaks, her amplified voice changes register electronically till her range and texture is that of an old man. As* SHE *speaks,* SHE *sheds the vestiges of the woman — earrings, wig, jeweled teeth.*

Alexander Lujak was seventy-one
When he killed himself with a deer rifle
In the bedroom of his home. It was raining

His daughters had left him
One for a black man, the other for a Jew
A first son and namesake, aged two
Had drowned in an irrigation ditch

He left the church

Twenty-eight years later a second son
Childless, had had himself vasectomized
Which terminated descent through the male line

His wife, Nettie, having
Undergone shock treatments
Was now institutionalized

The previous year he had suffered
A pulmonary edema and had actually died
For sixty seconds. In the last months
Try as he may he could not stop smoking

The PERFORMER *puts on the mask and assumes the character of Alex Lujak. The memory, in prerecorded video images, of Alex and his daughter preparing to journey by truck accompanies the narration. Twice, a closeup of the* PERFORMER *in the mask of Alex appears superimposed over an image of trapped water moving under a sheet of ice.*

Despite his Polish name he was a Croat
Born in Ruma, Yugoslavia, July 6, 1912
The second of four, he emigrated with his parents
To a small farm near Cleveland, Ohio
Married in 1937, with a grammar school education
He worked in a steel mill during the second World War
Contracting, as a result, severe bronchiectasic,
His lungs inflamed and weakened

From inhaling small bits of steel
He set out in 1947 in an old Army truck
With the family furniture piled in the back
For the clean air of the desert around
Phoenix, Arizona

    Taking with him
    His daughter, age eight
    For company

    He arranged the
Family furniture in the back of the truck
Just as it had been in her room at home
So she would not be afraid to go to sleep
When they stopped by the side of the road

The memory imagery shows the truck pulling off the road and entering the crypt-like cave that we saw earlier through the windshield of the careening truck before the sound of the gunshot. The truck in the enormous cave — like the entrance to a mine — travels with its lights on. Then stops by a rock wall. The FATHER, *his face never once seen, lifts the sleeping* CHILD *from the cab and puts her in her own bed in the back of the truck. We see the arrangement of the furniture as has been described. We see the figure of the* FATHER *take up the deer rifle and prepare to sit up all night guarding the* CHILD — *tapping the gun strangely with his fingernail. Slowly, we pull back to show* FATHER, CHILD, *gun and room inside the truck inside the grave. The* PERFORMER *in the mask continues to speak with an old man's voice, but subtly it starts to change and evolve back into her own.*

Late in life, with doubts and fears
As to the wisdom of his actions
After a son was born and the
Father and the daughter were estranged
He gave to her a sum of money
As a loan — for him so great a sum
That the amount was never mentioned in the home

It was spoken of as forty dollars
As one speaks of forty days and nights
Of flooding, or of wandering for forty years

Unfortunately, fate conspired
To prevent repayment
Before death intervened

Unfortunately, Alexander Lujak
Died afraid of being cheated

The PERFORMER'*s voice is now completely her own.*

O primitive man
Hunter, Fisher
Gatherer of spare parts
Who dies not of love
Dies of shame

I love this room
I want to die in this room
And I would, had not I had
The need to do you
      Poetic justice

Had not I owed you
This guarding of your dying, now
The way you guarded, then
      My sleeping

Jealously

Jealously I sing of you, Alex
Who I killed, (of course I did)
You are the death that sets my living free
You are my impossibility

The electronically created old man's voice suddenly takes over
again.

I love this room
I want to die in this room
And I would, had not I heard
This call to pilgrimage
This knot of God in my throat
Drop of God on my eyelash
This deep dreaming home
Where you're waiting . . . dancing

The PERFORMER *in the mask dances the dance of pilgrimage against the "rain of memory" in the mirrors to the ecstatic music of the end of* The Mawlid-Invocation of the Divine Name. *At the conclusion of the dance,* SHE *faces the audience and rips the latex mask in half. Half remains clinging to her face. Half* SHE *throws down.*

> *I want to kill and love*
> *In the identical motion*
> *In the identical word*
> *In the identical devotion*

I want not one impossible thing, but two
Out of not one impossible need, but two
Called not one impossible name, but two
I am not one impossible one, but two

Here in the dark box of my throat I bring you back to life

> *I rip you off . . .*

SHE *rips off the remaining portion of the mask.*

> *. . . for all to see*
> *Just how alive a corpse can be*

> *In my body, Alexander*
> *Your charmed bones*
> *Take on a certain glow*

The PERFORMER *returns to the dressing table, puts on her robe and puts cold cream on her cheeks.*

You can't leave me; that plan has a flaw
We'll never sort each other's atoms out
We are under sentence of a Boyle's law
For hope's dispersal in chambers of doubt

The lights go out.

END

44.   Call and response is alive and well and living in Africa. It is the missing link. But you won't find it in the Olduvai. You'll find it in the Studio Phonodisk, Lagos, Nigeria, or at the Club Sahel in Dakar, and in most African colonies such as Warner Bros. Records on Jack Warner Blvd. in Burbank. Perhaps over the same roots two trees grow. Perhaps call and response is also the missing link in the evolution of *performance* — a force that passes culture over distance and through time.

45.   *A Little Organon of the Theatre* would have us divide theatrical time into "A.B" and "B.B" ("A.B." — After Brecht — characterized by the *verfrumdungseffekt* and "B.B." by *empathy*). When you emotionally identify, when you are moved, yours is the way of catharsis. We, we post-Cartesians, have a decorous image of empathy, the "crying at the sad parts and the smiling at the glad parts" — but there are more potent forms of empathy.

46.   Response is performed empathy. How could anyone mistake it? Listen to the wolves.

47.   Let's go back to kindergarten. Here is a "turned wolf." Her name is Miss Simpson. Here is the howling, wolfish word, but it is called Jack in the Beanstalk. She calls to us, this teacher, this preacher, this Homer, this shaman, this griot. All together now, "Fi! Fie! Fo! Fum!" — we answer as one. We are a chorus, we wolves, we maenads, we chanting monks, we back-up singers, we thespians, we kindergartners. It remains for us to turn around. O were the *art* to propagate by ever larger groups of callers turning to ever more responders in the motion of a wave.

48.   Did not Jean Genet say imitation was love? Could it follow then that as empathy becomes love, response becomes mimesis? (Of course, if it's love, it's hate. See #22. But that's assumed, isn't it? I mean, who can trust a Genet?) O were *love* to propagate etc. (see *ART*, #47).

49.   Call and response is the living ancestor of choral drama. I can't prove it. I propose it. I bluff.

50.   Corollary to the proposition: In the days when people sang to one another, speech was music. Let's make theatre history. Here's a scenario. The Al Adan Al Chari comes to central Africa. Religious music mixes with religious music. The long melismatic

solo vocal line from the minaret joins the call and the response and percussion. The lead singer emerges. Long ago in Macedonia, did that solo singer sing a goat song?

51.   A primal tonal language of theatre has divided into speech and song. Choir is chorus, caller — choragos, singer — actor. Where is the orchestra? In the meter. Meter is the memory of where drums used to go. The ornamentation in the Muezzin's call — now we hear it in the "notches" of Afro-American lead singing. In the speaking mode, this is oratory, declamation, the "heightening" of language on the classic stage, Duse and Bernhardt. This is what gets you thrown out of the Actors Studio. Are we up to Aeschylus, O Dramaturgy?

52.   Palms won't grow in the mountains. Pines won't grow by the tropical seas. Can you, O Dramaturgy, see the roots for the branches as easily as the forest for the trees? Roots are soil-specific. You can't put them down just anywhere. A social soil is what a theatre feeds on. One tree's feast is another tree's poison.

53.   Did you catch *Britannicus* at the National Theatre of Haiti? It must be running now. Logic demands it — logic that holds a nation's classics to be a function of a nation's language. Isn't Racine just the epitome of the Haitian sensibility? Is not Racine to Haiti as Shakespeare to America?

54.   Here we have not planted, we have transplanted. How can the transplant live in a changed society? It no longer knows the language. Where can it grow in the uncommunicative soil? In a hothouse.

55.   Empirical Yankee, you are still a colonial on the stage. Britain, you parody of power, your puppet despots still reign in Academia, and their chiefs of police sit at the drama desks of the most influential newspapers in the Western world.

56.   The Anglophile has made us anglophiliac.

57.   My daughter went to high school in Abijan in 1985 and studied dance with Marie Rose Gireaux, whose troupe was Yoruba. On a visit I played for Marie Rose Gireaux Clarence Fountain's preaching bridge in " A Voice Foretold" from *Gospel at Colonus*. She said it sounded like a funeral oration in her village in the Dan.

58.   Theatre's language comes up from the street and down from the church and meets. Noh comes down from Buddhist chanting, the Bunraku of Chikimatsu Monzain up from the Osaka tea houses; Shakespeareanisms come down from the

Anglican sermon and up from the "stews" on the Thames. In Latin Europe it is down from the Mass and up from Commedia dell'Arte. A new vernacular language like Dante's is the beginning of a cultural nation. There is a language like this in America — as different in spirit from King James's English as Dante's Italian from the Latin of the Church. It comes down from Baptist and Pentacostal preaching and up from the ghettos. Black oratory, like music, is a four-hundred-year-old Afro-European synthesis. Is it an Elizabethan English for the new world? At the moment it's drafting its history plays with the speeches of Jacksons and Kings.

59.   And this is just the "east side" story. In the West, Asia assimilates us. Alan Watts' importation of a parapsychological Buddha, minimal art, Ridley Scott's L.A.-Tokyo supercity, Bushido — economics, Bruce Lee. Asia assimilates us from the West as we assimilate Asia at a rate of population growth unheard of in our history. Which is very curious because we know culture is racist. That's just biology.

60.   Theatre is fighting a Hundred Years' War with art. The motivational tradition versus the formalist! What's *good* in one is *bad* in the other. *Good* performance is *bad* acting. *Good* acting is *bad* performance. *Dramatic* time is cornball art. Abstract imagery is *arty* theatre. *Psychology* is too personal for art. *Conceptual art* is too intellectual for theatre. This is an unholy war. Where theatre is still holy it is still necessary. Aesthetics shrivel in the pure light of necessity.

61.   Brazil! Trinidad! You who have your theatres rolling and dancing through the streets. In our mausoleums at the Kennedy and Lincoln Centers we hear you, faintly.

62.   *The Warrior Ant:* on one side there is Babatunde Olatunji, who drums and narrates; on another, Yoshida Tamamatsu puppeteers; and on the third, Bob Telson and I write words and music. We hope this triangle is roughly equilateral. It's not hip enough to be really fashionable, but then again, it's too three-sided to be really square.

63.   In #22 I mentioned that the killer force and lover force are volatile — that alone they burn, mixed they explode. Well, around that explosion sits an audience in a ring. And if that theatre is going somewhere, the circle flattens out to a long thin shape like a worm. And the leader of the pack — that wolf known as the Pied Piper — leads us all out of town and down the garden path. And the shape of the performance is a parade. And it's Fat Tuesday, and hearing is cheering. And this is the *dance*.

The 1986 work-in-progress production of *The Warrior Ant* at Lincoln Center in New York, from top to bottom: puppet master Yoshida Tamamatsu with puppet "Princess Kuzunoha" assisted by Kevin Davis; Drums of Passion; Los Pleneros de la 21.

The Warrior Ant

The Warrior Ant *(parts I and XII of a planned epic-scale work) was produced by Liza Lorwin as a work-in-progress on June 16, 1986 at Alice Tully Hall, Lincoln Center for the Performing Arts, New York City. It was presented by the Composers' Showcase series, Charles Schwartz, artistic director, and by Lincoln Center. Poems, lyrics and staging were by Lee Breuer, and music and musical direction by Bob Telson. Musical groups featured were Little Village (Sam Butler and Margaret Dorn, vocals); Los Pleneros de la 21; Empire Loisaida Escola de Samba; Drums of Passion; and the Brooklyn Institutional Radio Choir (Carl Williams, Jr., director).* The Warrior Ant *featured Babatunde Olatunji as narrator and percussionist, and Yoshida Tamamatsu of the Bunraku Gekijo as master puppeteer.*

The Voice of the Queen was Ruth Maleczech; the Voice of the Warrior Ant, Lute Ramblin'; the Voice of the Death Moth, Leslie Mohn; and the Voice of the Termite, Ron Vawter.

The Warrior Ant and the Death Moth were portrayed by the puppets Kotaro and Princess Kuzunoha of the National Puppet Theatre of Japan. They were created by Ohe Tatunosuke, a "National Treasure." Yoshida Tamamatsu's puppeteers were Barbara Pollitt, Steven Kaplin and Kazuko Takai, assisted by Chris Odo, Kevin Davis and Mariko Ohsawa. Costume and puppet maintenance was by Kazuko Takai. Puppet choreography was under the direction of Tamamatsu, assisted by Barbara Pollitt.

Puppet stage paintings and design were by Alison Yerxa; puppet stage structural design by Daniel Ptacek with Thomas Ptacek; sound by Rock City Sound, Shelton Lindsay with Paul Antonell; lighting by Julie Archer. Sal Rasa was production stage manager, Ghretta Hynd was costume consultant, and the company manager was Frier McCollister.

I

An Ant Conceived

It is projected that the performance be a carnival parade, each "hour" or prayer manifested by a musical band or float or pageant wagon entering, circling, disappearing. The actors on their special stage (like a reviewing box) tell the story. Gigantic flower stems and blades of grass reduce the paraders to the size of ants.

A CHOIR enters and sings:	*Of you, O Warrior Ant, we sing.* *Father of nations!* *Builder of hills.*
	Of you, O Warrior Ant, we sing.
The GRIOT speaks over the choir:	Conqueror of Peanut Brittle,

Oracle of the moon-ribbed cricket's
   chirp, who, at the calling
   of a chemistry known as

Destiny's Marinade, waged
   ravenous and holy war ten years.
   Its names were Peppercorn of God!

And Lord of Millimeter!
   Hear of its birth, which
   was no less than miraculous!

The CHOIR concludes:

Of you, O Warrior Ant, we sing.
Hear of its birth
A miracle
On the night of the flight of Virgin Queens.

**And exits. Noon light. The
GRIOT with an instrument
chants and plays:**

On the noon of the night of the flight
   of the virgin queens begins the
   to and the fro of the branches.

This swishing and bending — now
   here is the story — receiving and
   sending, this thing of the calling —

Calling one to another:
   the callings by names and the
   callings of branches, to and fro

The *yes* and the *no,* that be nameless.
   O callings be nameless!
   O beautiful things!

**The GRIOT chants and
dances:**

O rain! O spontaneous sweet
   rising rain! O afternoon before
   the night the queens take flight!

The falling rain is as a curtain drawn
   across the rising rain, the rising rain
   is like a fountain in a cloud.

And like a juice upon the surfaces,
   a pool in the interstices —
   a juice, a pool, a fountain —

They appear so lovingly, the
  drops of the wetness are said to
  succor . . .

On the leaf and the fold does this
  wetness *succor;* on each pistil and
  petal — the drops of this wetness.

All parts of the earth smell of juices;
  each drinks down the other, when the
  drops of the wetness are said to *succor.*

A BOMBA BAND enters. It
plays, sings, and dances:

All parts of the earth
Smell of juices

Each drinks down the other
A juice, a pool, a fountain

Rain, sweet rising rain, falling rain
Like a fountain in a cloud

Afternoon before the night
The night the queens take flight

All parts of the earth
Smell of juices

And exits

GRIOT:

Here is the moment the light is divided
  I speak of the twilight, before flight
  and the thing of the choosing.

Twilight. MUSICIANS with
mbira and percussion enter
and sing:

The glow of the likeness
The gleam from the darkness

O strands of sun with
Strands of moonlight streaming.

Called light of lights and
Lights of seeming
Twilights beaming.

I speak of the wanting
I speak of love's haunting

Mouth to mouth like
Colored juices flowing.

In this the moment
Of the rain's bowing.

The hearing of wings
Virgins in flight
The nearing of wings
Virgin queens
Bless'd be your night

And exit

GRIOT:

In the heart of the night of the
    flight of the virgin queens begins
    the beatings;

**A SAMBA DRUMMER enters
and solos**

                 the black beatings
With the colors of the auras ringed
    around.

**Another DRUMMER enters
and solos**

        Begins the notes . . .

**Another DRUMMER enters
and solos**

                  Ah!
The notations.

**Another DRUMMER enters
and solos**

       And the poems! O poems . . .

**Another DRUMMER enters
and solos. The SAMBA SCHOOL
enters drumming and
singing:**

Such as thou art
Thou art rubbings, scrapings and gnashings
Such as thou art
The oowheeging, claxing, tintinking
Such as thou art
Thou art love's floatings and flyings
Such as thou art
Thou art love's heart

In the heart of the night
Of the flight of the Virgin Queens
Begins the black beatings
The notes, notations, poems
The forms such as they are
Hear them perform

In the heart are the forms
The oohs and the aahs
They are the percussions
In concert through the realm
Secret expressions

Such as thou art
Thou art love's heart

SAMBA SCHOOL **exits**

GRIOT:

The secrets are most perfectly spoken of
as a speechlessness. Heard as silence.

O thou, silence — thou art love's
roaring of mind. But thou, O black bleatings —
Such as thou art, thou art love's heart.

**Night. A float enters. Upon
it is depicted the pageant of
the wall of pain**

Now, it is common knowledge that the
edge of night's surrounded by a wall
of pain. But it is uncommon knowledge

**An ACTRESS on the narration
stage speaks over music:**

That the wall is peach. Peach
is the color of the blood of angels.
And it is common knowledge

That love, that night, this discourse,
with such a wall as I've described,
acts like a prison. But it is

Uncommon knowledge that the prison's
fleshy . . . peach and fleshy.
There are white windows in these walls;

**A window appears in the
dark wall of pain.
Simultaneously, the moon
rises**

They are round and holy and they
pour forth light, and at the center
of each window is its dark gleam.

And it is not knowledge at all
    but an intuition, a secret, and a
    divining, that one can love

With such a power on this night
    that one can rise and
    hover high upon the wall,

That one can see right through
    a window in the wall of pain.
    One can see through it!

**The wall in the moonlight
appears to be a face**

Beloved! I speak not of walls
    but of faces like walls,
    high-boned peach fortresses.

(Peach is the color of the blood
    of angels.) A window in a wall of pain
    is an eye in the face of a beloved

And the gleam in the eye
    is the refraction of a flame
    of recognition in a heart below.

Around each dark gleam eyes pour forth
    a light beam. And as in no other
    beam of light, each wave and quanta

Goes not thither at all impossible speed
    but calls to the darkness, "O come hither,
    darkness, in your impossible need."

**The moon grows larger.
Three SINGERS on the float
sing to it:**

*O shadow, O mother, O stronger
    than me, you are the soul's
    self-same dichotomy.*

*On the breast in a shadow of weakness
    lie; in a buckle of knees
    and a turning of ankles, fly.*

*Yea, though he walk, he falters.
    Yea, though he run, he falls back
    in the true arms of love.*

O power, O lover, O deep
  mystery, you are desire's
  impossibility.

In the true arms, loved and lover
  wonder, "Who is holding you? Whose
  is the third arm under?"

Yea, though he walk, he falters.
  Yea, though he run, he falls back
  in the true arms of love.

**The float exits. Three
narrators appear,
representing the** QUEEN, **the**
TERMITE, **and the** WARRIOR **as
a child.**

QUEEN: The night of flight of virgin queens
                 is love in the eye of the beholder.

TERMITE: And love in the eye of the beholder

               Is death in the eye of the beheld.
                 I speak for the drone, now,
                   the beholder whose art is suicide.

QUEEN: How does it prepare its mind?

WARRIOR: It prepares its mind in the way of
               lightness;

TERMITE: it thrusts from its mind

WARRIOR: The weight of consequence.

QUEEN: I speak
               for the drone, now, whose colors are

WARRIOR: cerise in blue:

TERMITE: a life reflective
               In a mode

WARRIOR: voluptuous,

QUEEN: a life

WARRIOR: incestuous

QUEEN: a

WARRIOR: childish life,

TERMITE: a life of

WARRIOR: art.

QUEEN: I speak for the drone.
                    for the beholder whose art is

WARRIOR: suicide.

TERMITE: The materials of this art are not expensive,
                    the apprenticeship not long. Masters —
                there have been but few.

                And they, scattered and little known.
                    Charlatans, fakirs, mere craftsmen —
                these have multiplied.

QUEEN: Yet even so

                The art of suicide has always ruled
                    the others. It rules over poetry. It
                    conquers music and vanquishes the dance.

The QUEEN **and the** TERMITE
together: It is said of this art — whose name
                    is *surrender*, that it is like
                    the cherry blossom over the blue wave;

                So frail that it shivers even before
                    the storm, and seeks to fall
                    even before the elements dislodge it,

                So as to give to the puff of wind
                    its fragrance, even as it gives
                    to the blue wave its flowery soul.

TERMITE:	All that has been writ is writ
	    here of the beholder, a warrior
	    of the caste of drone.
	
	An artist in its right,

WARRIOR:	a smaller life,
QUEEN:	when one considers the multitude in the scheme.
GRIOT:	And the ant says

WARRIOR:	I sing of the moment of the love
	    of *it* that was *our* last beginning
	    for once-and-for-all time.

**A JUJU BAND enters on a
bandwagon**
	*In the dead of night, in the secret
	    pocket of delight, I am borne
	    to be born. I am the permissions.*

**In a sequence of puppetry,
the flight of the virgin
queens is seen against the
enormous moon**
	*I am! In the laser of an eye. I am!
	    a white star seeding the black sky.
	    Remember the to and fro*

**The flight of the drones is
seen approaching them**
	*Of the branches — sending and receiving?
	    Even then and there, secretly,
	    I sang of my conceiving.*
	
	      *I am A Warrior Ant. Huh!
	      I am A Warrior Ant. Huh!*

WARRIOR:	Hooray! Here is a song
	    of celebration! "It is coming!
	    A warrior is coming!"
	
	All the angels cry, and all
	    flowers fly home to perfume the air.
	    "O welcome to me!"
	
	And "O welcome to me!" again!
	    I have begun us again in
	    a torrent and a blessedness

The spectacle of loving is played out over the sounds of a battle in the skies

On the night of the flight of
   the virgin queens there was borne
   to be born a warrior ant,

Perfect in the measure of its means.
   Here follows its history:
   Angels bore him to me, and now

Angels have borne him away. I was
   his soldier, yes, that was me.
   I was his spit, yes, and his polish.

I was his nib. And as his nib
   dipped in his spit and polish,
   I write you secrets of a language lost

And strategies for wars undreamed.
   May the light of the kingdoms —
   animal, vegetable, and mineral,

The drones fall, dead

And Gods, yes, God's little light
   shine down to console me.
   He blew me away. Yes, he did.

The bandwagon exits

XII

An Ant Concludes

The musicians of Part I horseshoe the stage. Center and raised above them, a Bunraku puppet stage. A backdrop of four large painted panels. The center two slide so as to appear and disappear from behind the outer two. Four low rectangular panels form the downstage playboard.

The CHILD NARRATOR (voice of the WARRIOR) speaks over a musical introduction:

An Ant alone is an ant afraid.
   It disappears and reappears
   like a sun flash on a water wave.

As each of us is seen by death,
   so draw a picture of an ant alone
   for fear of vanishing holding its breath.

**The ENSEMBLE plays and
sings:**

*An ant alone
is an ant afraid
it goes into this world
only to pray*

*An ant alone
Is an ant afraid
Holding its breath
So it won't blow away*

*It's looking for its mother
And finding her not
To God it turns
One God or another, saying*

*Take me, Lord, I want to be
smaller my God, to thee*

GRIOT:

To the naked eye an ant appears
   unchanged; but unto itself,
   it's metamorphosized. To the naked eye,

The music fades

It is a solid form; but unto itself
   it liquifies. An ant prays
   so fervently, it turns into a tear.

**The Bunraku puppet KOTARO
enters, manipulated by three
puppeteers. KOTARO and the
voice of the CHILD NARRATOR
represent the WARRIOR ANT.
Poses, changes of the
painted backdrops on the
sliding screens, significant
gestures, important lines
and changes of mood are
emphasized by percussion in
the Japanese tradition**

The campaign was over and
   the ant prepared to go home.
   Then it stopped short!

**The ANT is walking. A pose
of the ANT stopping short**

Not knowing where home was,
   The mist on the ground lifted and
   before the ant stood an incredible tree.

**IT leans backward to see the
tree's top**

The face of the tree was black.
   The sun behind it poured thick beams
   over all its trunk and branches.

The ANT kneels to pray

The ant rose on its hind legs
   It lifted its four hands in prayer
   and testified.

The voice of the ANT:

King of Kings and Lord of Plants!
   I am neither fish nor fowl;
   I am an insect!

Nowhere is home! No place!
   No person! I have fought ten years
   and nothing is won or lost.

Yet, I cannot say,
   "I fought for nothing!"
   I fought for You.

**The ANT trembles with fear
and covers its eyes**

When night fell upon my life
   I trusted it. I knew it
   to be your shadow. I have lived

Long among the dark temptations.
   I have lived with the Devil.
   (The Devil is the shadow of the Lord.)

**IT uncovers its eyes and
gazes in rapture**

And I sought false comforts. But
   I can see, on the other side of you
   light shines. I can see this!

The narrator is the QUEEN:

And with this, the ant cut off
   its antennae and took its vows.
   It vowed to go on pilgrimage

**The ANT takes off its sword
and its headband**

To the top of the Sequoia tree;
   higher than it had ever flown.
   It needed nothing; no staff, no

**The ANT poses at the foot of
the Sequoia tree**

Two screens slide into place
with a painting of an ant's
view of a Sequoia tree. The
climbing music begins. The
ANT climbs the Sequoia tree.
Twice, new paintings are
introduced showing the
height of its progress. The
GRIOT chants:

Bell, no bowl, no book. For thirst
   there were dewdrops; for the hunger
   of the Termite there was the body of the God.

The WARRIOR has reached
the top of the Sequoia tree
and gazes in awe. The CHOIR
sings:

At the topmost reaches of
   the Sequoia tree, the world is
   profound beyond intelligence.

Here! O Ant, here at this height!
   Here is the truth in the form
   of moisture! Here is a resound

Of thunder, and an enlightenment
   of rain, and here in each
   cloud is its proper cruelty.

In the blue light! In the blast
   of blue sky-lidded light, (which
   is inspiration), you will find

Your monastery hanging by a
   silken thread. Here, O Ant, life
   hangs by threads! Abide, O Ant,

And leave this world! Live out
   your life in this cocoon and here
   await the white moth of the moon.

The puppet PRINCESS
KUZUNOHA enters. SHE and
the voice of the female
narrator represent the DEATH
MOTH:

Abide it does and lives with Death
   in her pavilion in the sky until the
   time writ in the book for it to die.

SHE appears wrapped in a
cocoon of white silk hanging
by a thread from a branch.
SHE is unwound to the

music of a danza. The
narrator is the QUEEN:

And so a death moth becomes the
　　ant's last lover. Death and the Warrior!
　　Love is perfection, perfection of loves

Loved before; for of all the graces
　　and delights of passions past,
　　at core, what had not been

Death in them had been superfluous.
　　In Death there was no competition,
　　no contest for the goods of this world.

Death's needs were not in the
　　realm of the goods. She hungered not
　　for fame, fortune, or victory.

She was no searcher after self.
　　How strange! She was the antithesis
　　of all things ant-like. Yea —

As things create their opposites,
　　the insect's death was born of the excess
　　of life in it. As lover can discover

In itself, the self that is beloved,
　　as one embracing arm can feel its strength
　　according to the other's pressure —

So, to the ant, it was revealed
　　that Warriors exist
　　because Death loves them.

The narrator is the TERMITE:

What percentage of a falsehood

Is as good as true? What part of fact is
　　just one's faith in it? The power of an
　　ant's obsession rules summer's last days.

The MOTH **sits on a branch,**
stretching luxuriously

The insect erects a tower of euphoria.
　　(There is no upper limit to a
　　tower of euphoria.) Life and Death,

Here, in the form of ant and moth,
  work against time. They will conceive
  new generations; they will mount

New campaigns, command new armies;
  (Not of ants alone! Of half the
  insect world! And of some vertebrates!)

The ant will heal its wounds. Miraculously,
  new antennae from its brow will sprout,
  and wings, again, will lift it high as aether.

The cocoon becomes a shrine called
  The Pavilion on the Lake of Sky.
  Artists come and paint its holy history

On screens; these, in turn, in triptych,
  become ant ikons. *"Blessed are the Last Days*
  of Summer in the Pavilion on the Lake of Sky."

This is the title of the first screen.
  It shows Death, a late riser,
  basking in the sun as is her habitude;

On a green leaf, framed in the redwood
  branches, she drinks a delicious cup of coffee.

Blessed are the last days of summer
In the pavilion

On the lake of Sky
Basking in the sun
She drinks a cup of coffee

Her wings are black silk
The moth is night's snowflake

She opens her eyes
She whispers come fly with me

Blessed are the last days of summer
In the pavilion

The MOTH swims in the
blue air

    They go swimming high
    In the deep blue sky
First breaststroke   *Just like the birds, they're flying*

Then backstroke   *The time love can buy*
    Is time out from dying

THEY drink a champagne
toast, clinking glasses   *Let's drink to the sun*
    For winter lies waiting

MOTH and ANT exit together,
swimming   *Blessed are the last days of summer*
    In the pavilion

Spoken over music. The
narrator is the QUEEN: With love, it does not matter — day or
       night! Only flight matters. In these
       chosen hours, when, like orbed miracles,

    Sun and moon shine together, ant and moth
       step out upon the meniscus curve
       of blue, depressing the sky's skin

    Like bugs, the skin of water. They fly
       into the blooms of galaxies and suck the
       nectar therefrom. Yes, that is their food —

    The firestorms, the drops that burn
       like comets on the tongue. Love of moth
       is love of ant's apotheosis.

    Death is its darling; this Death is
       its own. Her wings, like two fellatio tongues,
       suck out its battlesongs and swallow.

    Sweet soft core of inspiration! Now
       it knows! Death gets it off! Of course,
       the ant is mad (and a trifle sexist, too).

    A Warrior, it confuses loving Death
       with conquering the thing.
       Yes, it confuses them . . .

THE WARRIOR ANT

Night. Moon. The
MUSICIANS play and sing: *Of the curse called "Love of Death"*
So much has been written
And on the death of love,
Even more
But what of the pain Death
Herself endures
For a living thing
Each time she takes one

The MOTH enters, weeping   *She cries until the clouds*
Are burnt through by starlight
Leaving him she flies off
Like a ghost
Only to reappear with a
host of golden trumpeteers
Now the ant can tell
Death is an angel

The ANT enters, asleep,
curled on a branch   *The warrior dreams*
She comes back to find him
The moth says to the ant
"I am truth!
And truth I fear
You don't want to hear"
The ant says, "Yes I do.
Death moth I want you."

The MOTH, weeping
profusely, lets down her hair *Each time she takes one*
Each time she takes a life
Into her heart
The rush of blood and
The flood of mind destroy her
Each time she takes one
Death dies a little too

The voice of the DEATH
MOTH over the music
continued instrumentally: Each time she takes a life into

Her heart, her heart breaks over it.
　　And broken-hearted she is brought, by stages,
　　to unbearable loneliness and decline.

The мотн performs what is
described, in the manner of
a dumb show

The moth becomes a recluse.
   She falters and fades, languishing
   like a flower deprived of sun and water.

Only rarely does she speak,
   and then, with such a childlike and
   tremulous sound, the ant hears it

As the music of a harp of cobwebs
   dripped upon by dews. By day
   she cowers wide-eyed with confusion,

Her mind a litany of anguish
   and a sensibility deranged.
   "What should she wear?"

"How should she do her hair?"
   The ant is seized with dread;
   he cannot find her thread.

sнe begins to choke and
tremble

By night her eyes are wider still
   for as confusion starts to clear,
   the moth begins to suffocate with fear.

The pit is deep; its walls are slippery.
   She lives with terror in a trance.
   Her need for love is endless,

(Fear burns love as a fiery fuel
   and the fires of the Death Moth
   are ever near extinguishing.)

What could Death be afraid of?

A pose of the мотн, grieving

GRIOT:

Alas, no thing can see with greater
clarity than she, that love will lose . . .

The мотн touches the ANT,
who awakens

Her wisdom comes upon her
   in an effect so curious; the
   moth dissolves in waves of light.

sнe takes it in her arms

Death's dear face is insubstantial;
   her body waxes and wanes, it becomes
   translucent, and the ant sees through her.

THEY **look into each other's eyes**

The ant sees right through Death.
 So rare a sight is this, so few
 of all the living things have

Seen this that an insect sees.
 The ant can see the angel which
 an eye must look through Death to see.

It sees Death is of God's dominion,
 too, not an unholy thing;
 God's creature, too, is Death.

THEY **weep together**

And the ant knows it shall die
 of pity. The story goes,
 "An Ant shall die of pity and love

The DEATH MOTH **carries the WARRIOR away**

For Her whom all the Saviors missed."
 O Compassionate Ant! How fitting!
 Death shall kill thee with her pain.

All the MUSICIANS **and** SINGERS **sing and play:**

O Warrior Ant
All wars are lost
Your luck's run out and
Ghostly storms are raging

O Warrior Ant
Who does she love
While you're dreaming
Which one is she taking

Fool
You loved her so dearly
You have won her
Awake and flee

O Warrior Ant
All wars are lost
Dreamy victories
Cannot redeem you

The music continues

O Warrior Ant
All wars are lost

There comes a night when even angels
   cannot sleep. They cry till all the
   clouds are burnt with falling stars.

On this night, Death, weeping, leaves
   the sleeping ant, and flies off like a ghost,
   into the moon; to reappear with minions.

O Ant! By day they're black as ash.
   By night, they're white, so you can
   see them in the sky without God's light.

The moth says to the ant,
   "I am the truth! And truth,
   I fear, you don't want to hear."

The ant says in its dream,
   "I do. Death Moth, I want you."
   And wedded to him by his words,

It's Death alights right on the leaf
   from which the tiny white cocoon
   hangs swaying. Inside, as in a holy cell,

The ant is sleeping. And the Gods
   in their Realms, and the beings on
   their planets ALL STOP EVERYTHING!

The wheel of Karma pauses till the truth
   be known. Can an ant attain enlightenment?
   Will the Warrior be the first among its kind?

**EVERYONE on stage shakes
his/her head sadly:**

No.

GRIOT:

O Ant, you'll wake no longer to this world.
   May you awake upon the fingernail of the Almighty!
   May you carry your crumb of Heaven home.

**The MOTH has awakened the
WARRIOR to DEATH**

Death claims the Warrior Ant
   for he is now her own. Like two
   dreams dreaming of each other,

**High against the night
clouds we see DEATH flying,
the ANT riding upon her
back as in a trance**

Ant flows into moth, moth into ant,
   across the line of void, until each
   annihilates the other with annihilating love.

The Death Moth and the Warrior Ant,
　　like the touching of a plus and
　　minus charge, vanish in mid-air.

For a moment the ANT
appears to hear the SINGERS
calling

And nature returns to herself,
　　and in its own mysterious way,
　　is tranquil. In the brittle bowl

Then its head falls back and
DEATH carries the WARRIOR
into another world

That holds this summer's passions
　　in a liquid form, a crack appears;
　　The mold breaks. Summer of the Insects!

O you tiny drops of joys and
　　even smaller sorrows — you leak away,
　　leaving earth's autumn as a residue.

END

About the Author   Lee Breuer was born in 1937, grew up in Los Angeles and attended U.C.L.A. He began to write and direct in San Francisco in the early sixties, and then lived in Europe and North Africa. In 1970 he co-founded Mabou Mines and began the performance poem *Realms*, a work in six parts. Parts I, II and III – the "animations" *Red Horse, B. Beaver* and *A Dog's Life (Shaggy Dog)* – were published in 1979. Part IV, *A Prelude to Death in Venice*, was published in 1982 and is reprinted here along with sections 1 and 12 of Part V, *A Warrior Ant*. Excepting *A Dog's Life*, this volume contains Lee Breuer's collected performance poetry for the decade 1976-1986. In 1983 he adapted Robert Fitzgerald's version of Sophocles' second Theban play, and with Bob Telson developed it as the musical work *The Gospel at Colonus*. Lee Breuer co-chairs the directing department at Yale University's School of Drama.